Precious C

This book was written for
the reader who feel trapped
by fear, insecurity & shame to
experience freedom through Gods
Word & love. It is my
own healing journey and
common ones my clients
have experienced. The lord loves
you & will bring you healing
& restoration.

Mari Plank

M000118199

MARI PLANK

STOP DANCING
WITH THE
ENEMY

copyright 2020 by Mark Plank

Cover Design by BookBaby

Published by Transformation Publishing

Westminster, Ca 92683

www.mariplanklifecoach.com

All Rights Reserved. No part of this publication may be reproduced, stored in a retrieval system, or transmitted in any form or by any means—for example, electronic, photocopy, or recording—without the prior written permission of the publisher. The Only Exception is brief quotations in printed reviews.

Print ISBN: 978-1-09832-286-1

eBook ISBN: 978-1-09832-287-8

Unless otherwise identified, scripture quotations are the New King James Version. www.crosswalk,com

TABLE OF CONTENTS

FORWARD

For several years, I have danced with *The Deceiver*, through low self- esteem, shame, guilt, fear, and abusive relationships. It felt like a prison with no way out. He led and I followed. I was depressed, hopeless, and weary of always feeling trapped.

Then I cried out to the Lord and he began to show me the power of His love and Word. As I began to dance with *The Beloved*, I discovered a newfound freedom, joy, and begin to experience His transformation and healing.

Isaiah 61 reflects His promise to set the captives free, open prison doors, and give joy for mourning. This is my prayer for my readers as they encounter *The Beloved*. His love will heal and transform! His Word will cut off the chains of *The Deceiver*. His precious daughters will reflect His glory!

INTRODUCTION

Beloved daughter of the Most High God, are you tired of limitation and fears? Are you feeling unloved, or do you question your worth and value? Do you desire freedom or courage? Would you like to know the depth and width of God's love? Do you desire to be set free from the past? Do you lack self-confidence, or are you trapped by shame and guilt? Do you feel bound? Imprisoned? Limited? Stuck? Hopeless? Have you answered "yes" to any of these questions? Then this book is for you. *Stop Dancing With The Enemy* will help you:

- Gain insight as to the source of your limitations and how to move with more freedom and power through God's Word and His love.
- Gain freedom over insecurity
- Understand how your identity in Christ will heal and transform
- Overcome past abuse
- Learn the powerful healing truth of God's love.
- Develop more confidence

- Defeat shame, guilt, and fear

Imagine you have come to watch the most exquisite dancers in the whole world. It is the grandest of all ballrooms. It is ornate and glorious in splendor. No detail overlooked. Her beautiful gown swirls around her feet, her hair and jewelry perfect. Look at her dance! Anyone that beautiful must not have any cares of this world. But her graceful movements and beauty are simply a cover-up for the truth.

Her partner greets and escorts her to the floor. He is wearing a tuxedo and appears to be the most handsome man ever. Appearance is deceiving and hides his true identity. *The Deceiver* has come to steal, kill, and destroy. He seems so inviting and such a skilled dancer. He knows exactly how to lead and direct her movements.

The audience is captivated by the exquisite performance. They clap and cheer as they execute difficult dance steps, spinning and twirling as one across the dance floor. Every step more intricate, every step synchronized perfectly to the music.

What they do not see are the chains that are shackled to her ankles. She spins around, and the chains wrap around her tightly, creating wounds at every turn. Her hands are chained to her partner. Every step becomes difficult, and the chains ensnare her soul, mind, and emotions. They are choking the life out of her, yet she continues to dance. She feels the strangulation of the shackles but continues to dance.

There is another one on the sidelines waiting to dance. His name is *The Beloved. The Healer, The Deliverer, The Prince of Peace. The Light.* He is dressed befitting a King. He is radiant and glorious. Tenderness, mercy, and compassion emanate from Him.

Sadly, we often leave *The Beloved* on the sidelines and find ourselves once again dancing with *The Deceiver.* It is what we know. We are seduced by his trickery, deceit and lies. We have exchanged the truth for his lies. We do not recognize the lies because they are familiar. We hear them echoing in our heart. "You are a failure," "You are weak," "and "You are nothing." We think they are just our own thoughts, and we continue to dance.

Precious,

My daughter, how I long to partner with you in the Dance of Freedom. I will give you joy, healing, and restoration. It is My heart's desire to lead you on the heavenly dance floor. Trust My love for you. Hear the tenderness in My heart toward you. Allow Me to cut off the chains that have shackled and bound you.

A PARTY OF THREE

Love letter from heaven:

Precious One,

How I long to dance with you. I want to remove your chains. I will teach you how to live through My grace. Let Me lead you into the dance of healing and freedom. Let Me lead you in the dance of My unconditional love and acceptance. I want My Spirit to be the wind beneath your feet. Come dance with Me! Whoever is in Me is free indeed!

* * *

Partner Dancing

In partner dancing there is one who will lead and one who follows. The lead determines the flow, direction, and tempo of the dance. He also may incorporate new steps. Some may also act as the choreographer who creates original dances and develops new interpretations of existing dances. They may demonstrate dance moves to instruct dancers in the proper technique.

There are two who desire to dance and direct our steps. Both want to lead, and we can choose whom to follow. One brings life and the other death. One wants to set free, and the other wants to imprison. One loves us with an everlasting love, and the other hates everything about us. One is the victor and the other defeated.

The thief does not come except to steal, and to kill, and to destroy. I have come that they may have life, and that they may have it more abundantly. John 10:10 .

The Beloved

His name is *The Beloved, Alpha and Omega, The Prince of Peace, the King of Glory, Redeemer, and Everlasting.* He is gentle and full of mercy, love, compassion, and acceptance. He desires to wrap you with robes of His righteousness. He sings over us with joy and gladness!

The Lord your God in your midst, The Mighty One, will save; He will rejoice over you with gladness, He will quiet you with His love, He will rejoice over you with singing. Zeph. 3:17

The Beloved is asking for your hand. He wants to lead you on His dance floor. Are you willing? Will you trust His lead? Will you allow Him to heal? Will you allow Him to remove the chains that have imprisoned your heart and soul?

He comes with healing in His wings. He will bring restoration, worth, and value. He reveals His eternal purpose and removes our grave clothes. His words are truth, healing, transformation, redemption, and restoration. He is passionate for us. His death and resurrection prove His love.

He gave us the ability to be transformed by the power of His love. His death and resurrection broke the power of *The Deceiver*. Through His Spirit, we can become more than overcomers.

Yet in all these things we are more than conquerors through Him who loved us. Rom 8:37

There is a longing in His heart for us to know Him deeper and dance like a King and His daughter. He speaks words of life, love, peace, healing, and restoration. We listen for a moment but turn a deaf ear because we are accustomed to the voice of *The Deceiver*.

The Deceiver

The Deceiver is the father of lies (see John 8:44). He is a source of wounds, offenses, hurts, abuse, and destruction. His plan is to steal, kill, and destroy everything *The Beloved* has for you. He will force his plan of destruction and desires to annihilate anything good or lovely in your life.

You are of your father the devil, and the desires of your father you want to do. He was a murderer from the beginning, and does not stand in the truth, because there is no truth in him.

ix

When he speaks a lie, he speaks from his own resources, for he
is a liar and the father of it. John 8:44

His voice is one of condemnation, ridicule, shame, and guilt. He reminds us of all our pain, mistakes, bad choices, and everything else that we've done wrong. *The Deceiver* is our prison guard and masterful with captivity. His voice is so subtle. When he speaks, we think it is our thoughts. He desires to create limitation, strip away our worth and value, and bring discouragement, doubt, and torment.

Dear ones, let's only choose to dance with *The Beloved* and be transformed by His love, life, grace, and mercy. Let us become daughters of *The Beloved. The Deceiver* comes to steal, kill, and destroy, and *The Beloved* gives us abundant life.

A thief is only there to steal and kill and destroy. I came so
they can have real and eternal life, more and better life than
they ever dreamed of. John 10:10 The Message Bible

In conclusion, it is easy to bounce between both partners. There are days when I dance with *The Beloved* and hear His sweet voice of grace and love. Other days I choose *The Deceiver* and dance with him. Shame, guilt, condemnation, unbelief, doubt, discouragement, and frustration overtake my soul. I find myself weighed down and bound with his chains.

I am starting to recognize when I am dancing with *The Deceiver*. And then I simply choose *The Beloved*. He graciously and lovingly extends His arms again and again to me.

What are the four foundational steps?

In every type of dance, whether it is hip-hop, ballet, ballroom, tap, jazz, or polka, there are steps that build a foundation. Once a dancer knows the foundational steps, they can add, modify, or create their own interpretation. Often, these steps have names such as

- Ball Change
- Box Step
- Chaîné Turns
- Toe to heel

There are four foundational steps that make up the *Dance of Freedom* at the end of each dance chapter. We will be taking one chapter for each foundational step and explain in detail how it works. In the *Dance of Freedom*, we will learn how to apply all of them for each chapter. Our four foundational steps are:

- Foundational Step 1: *Dance of Awareness*
- Foundational Step 2: *Dance of the Word*
- Foundational Step 3: *Dance of Lyrics*
- Foundational Step 4: *Dance of Forgiveness*

CHAPTER ONE

FOUNDATIONAL STEP 1: DANCE OF *AWARENESS*

Examine me, God, from head to foot; order your battery of tests. Make sure I am fit inside and out.
Psalm 26:2 The Message Bible

Love letter from heaven:

Precious One,

I desire to increase your awareness of how The Deceiver continually destroys your life through lack of understanding. Even though I broke the chains of death, sin, destruction, pain, suffering, and torment you remain bound through his deception and lies. Learn how My truth will set you free.

I desire for you to be a strong, healthy tree planted by My living water. You will bear fruit of truth, hope, love, confidence, and of My

Holy Spirit. I destroyed The Deceiver and humiliated Him on the cross. I made a public mockery of Him when I rose again. My truth or wisdom will protect and watch over you.

* * *

Precious and The Deceiver began their dance. Precious is unable to hear or see and is shrouded in complete darkness. She relies on The Deceiver to lead, tell her what to believe, what to think, and what to feel. This causes more destructive reactions and responses. Precious sees the rotten, decayed, withered fruit she is bearing. Her diseased trunk is nourished by roots deeply embedded in lies, pain, devastation, disappointment, fear, and loss. The Deceiver intentionally calculates every step for her devastation. The more Precious allows him to lead, the greater the entanglement and imprisonment become.

What is awareness?

Awareness is recognition, realization, cognizance, perception, apprehension, and understanding. Hosea 4:6 tells us that God's people perish for lack of knowledge. The Hebrew word for knowledge is "da'at." This means knowledge, knowing, understanding, intelligence, wisdom, discernment, and skills. In each chapter, we will apply this foundational step to the chapter. Through awareness the doors of revelation and healing will be opened.

Why is it foundational?

The Dance of Awareness is important because it helps us to understand the relationship between our attitudes, actions, emotions, and our belief system. Our beliefs are conscious and unconscious "truths" that we believe to be true. In the chapter *Dance of Lyrics* this is explained in detail.

Awareness: Know Your Tree

So, every healthy tree bears good fruit, but the diseased tree bears bad fruit. Matt. 7:17 ESV

A tree is a great illustration. Trees have fruit, trunk, and roots. Sickly or bitter fruit result from pests, diseases, or lack of proper soil or nutrients. Our fruit is what is seen on the outside. Our trunk or beliefs produce our fruit. The roots pull up whatever is in our soil. It nourishes the roots, trunk, and fruit.

God desires for us to be planted by the rivers of His water and will bring forth fruit in its season.

Blessed is the man who walks not in the counsel of the ungodly, nor stands in the path of sinners, nor sits in the seat of the scornful; but his delight is in the law of the Lord, and in His law, he meditates day and night. He shall be like a tree planted by the rivers of water that brings forth its fruit in its season , whose leaf also shall not wither; and whatever he does shall prosper. Ps. 1:1-5

Fruit. Fruit are attitudes, actions, emotions, behaviors, judgments, and perceptions. It reflects the nourishment it receives from the roots. The roots draw nourishment from the soil.

The trunk is our belief system or lyrics. The trunk is our belief system or lyrics and directly connects the roots with the fruit. It supports, protects, and nourishes the fruit.

The soil. The soil nourishes the entire tree through the roots. The fruit reflects the condition of the soil because it is draws up nutrients through the root system through the trunk and branches. We reflect what nourishes us as well.

Recognize the trunk

The trunk is our belief system and directly connects the roots with the fruit. It supports, protects, and nourishes the fruit. Later, we will refer to our trunk as "lyrics."

Definition: thoughts, ideas, values, opinions, judgments, views, principles, conviction. Your thoughts determine what you become.

> *"For as he thinks in his heart, so is he." "Eat and drink!" he says to you, but his heart is not with you.* Prov. 23:7

Renewed thoughts enable you to know God's good and perfect will. *Therefore, I urge you, brothers and sisters, by the mercies of God, to present your bodies [dedicating all of yourselves, set apart] as a living sacrifice, holy and well-pleasing to God, which is your rational* (logical, intelligent) act of worship. And do not be conformed to this world [any longer with its superficial values and customs], but be transformed and progressively changed [as you mature spiritually] by the renewing of your mind [focusing on godly values and ethical attitudes], so that you may prove [for yourselves] what the will of God is, that which is good and acceptable and perfect [in His plan and purpose for you]. Rom. 12:1, 2 The Amp. Bible

Examples of beliefs: (This is not God's good and perfect will for us to believe these)

- I do not belong. I will always be on the outside (l am left out).
- I do not believe God loves me unconditionally.
- My feelings do not count. No one cares what I feel.
- I am always afraid of rejection.
- I will isolate myself so that I will not be vulnerable to hurt, rejection. etc. anymore.
- I am not worthy to receive anything good from God.
- I am not good enough.
- I feel condemned.
- I am dirty, unclean.
- I am ashamed of myself.
- Something is wrong with me.
- I take care of myself because no one will.
- My addiction makes me feel…

- I am on my own, independent.
- It is difficult to have healthy relationships.
- It is uncomfortable to receive love.
- I keep everyone at a distance.
- I need control.
- I am quick to cut off relationships.
- I am codependent.
- I am unable to submit and trust authorities, and view authorities as a vehicle of hurt.
- I must perform.
- I am afraid
- I feel insecure.
- I do not have worth.
- I need to protect myself.
- I need to distance myself from God.

Recognize the soil

The soil feeds the roots that extract nutrients and nourishes the entire tree. Our soil can be culture, relationships, how we were raised, experiences, etc. Soil feeds our trunk or beliefs and then produces fruit. We cannot change our past, but we can change our trunk through the Word of God, resulting in good fruit such as peace, love, joy, self-control, patience, goodness, healing, deliverance, healthy relationships, etc.

My testimony:

Prior to my healing I was an emotional mess. Depressed, zero self-esteem, negative self-image, self-hater, constant fear of rejection and driven by performance. I was drawn to my husband who had similar emotional baggage. Domestic violence, codependency, and victimization created traumatic experiences for my children and me.

There were five years of dating and four years of a tumultuous relationship. Four times a year I would "run away" with my kids to temporary shelter with friends or family.

Prompted by promises of change, we would reunite. Things were okay for a short time, until escalation began, and the violence and trauma would happen repeatedly. The cycle repeated itself over time. During that time, the Lord was teaching me the "whys" of my victimization. Blaming my husband seemed perfectly justified since he was the perpetrator.

However, I had responsibility to learn "The Dance of Awareness." Awareness of how partners in domestic violence interacted. I had to understand my fruit, beliefs, the soil, and roots. God used this awareness and brought healing to many pervasive emotional and relational entanglements.

Over the course of time, God healed and delivered me. He restored my soul, healed my low self-esteem, caused me to understand my worth and value in Christ. My children and future grandchildren were spared from "inheriting" the trauma and sin of domestic violence.

In conclusion, *The Dance of Awareness* is the first foundational step in *Stop Dancing with the Enemy*. God's truth will set you free. God's love will heal worthlessness and low self-esteem and break cycles of abuse, self-hatred, and dysfunctional relationships. It will restore your heart, soul, and mind and allow you to dance with *The Beloved* as His precious daughter.

* * *

Dance with *The Beloved*

The Beloved offers Precious His hand, and they begin to dance. It is painful to see the fruit, lyrics, and roots that have caused so much pain. Unlike The Deceiver who shrouded her in darkness to keep awareness away, The Beloved's light wraps her awareness in grace, love, and hope. Where light is, there is healing and truth. Truth brings freedom. He shows her now as a tree planted by His living water. Her fruit reflects healing and restoration. There is assurance, confidence, love, and fruit of the Holy Spirit. Her trunk is healthy and strong through the Word.

Her roots are nourished by God's Love and His Power. The Beloved's desire to bring new awareness to Precious was motivated by His love. There was no condemnation. Even when she stumbles and falls back into the arms of The Deceiver, The Beloved is always there with open arms. He is always willing to dance again with Precious.

* * *

Dance your way to freedom! Envision yourself as the dancer.

https://mariplanklifecoach.com/dance-of-awareness/

CHAPTER TWO

FOUNDATIONAL STEP 2: DANCE OF THE WORD

How sweet are your words to my taste, Sweeter than honey to my mouth! Psalm 119:103

Love letter from heaven:

Precious One,

How I want you to learn My Dance of the Word. I desire My truth to be your foundation. I delight in showing you how to dance with grace and freedom. My Word is life-giving, healing, and it will transform your life. I desire for it to become deep-heart knowledge. I desire for you to be planted next to My living water and blossom as My beautiful flower. Drink in My Word. Allow its refreshing truth to wash away the decay and old ways.

* * *

Precious and The Deceiver begin to dance. The floor beneath them is crumbling, decayed, and treacherous, and there is no foundation beneath her feet. She is slipping into what feels like a dark abyss. Negative unspoken words of others and judgments are spiraling around, causing fear and condemnation. Her soul feels like the dark night of endless despair. The Deceiver's words are like shards of glass cutting her soul.

* * *

Why is this a foundational step?

Words have great power. They have the power to shape, influence, build, destroy, plant, and bring things into being. Consider what happened before creation. The earth was dark and empty, and God spoke, and creation occurred after He spoke.

> *In the beginning God created the heavens and the earth. Now the earth was formless and empty, darkness was over the surface of the deep, and the Spirit of God was hovering over the waters. And God said, "Let there be light," and there was light. God saw that the light was good, and he separated the light from the darkness. Gen. 1:1–2*

Creation progresses as God speaks,

…light

…separation of night and day

…division between land and sea

…vegetation, trees,

…moon and sun to govern night and day

…all animal life

…creation of mankind (man and women).

Just as God's Word has power to create, so the words we hear either spoken or unspoken have the impact to create, build, destroy, or influence us.. Do you remember hearing words that stuck with you? Did they cause damage to your soul, or did they impart encouragement?

We are often the byproduct of spoken or unspoken words. Our souls are often filled with wounds resulting from negative, harsh, or hurtful words. They are like fruit and will deposit their seeds and reproduce in our life. God's desire is for His Word to shape and influence us. This foundational step will be incorporated at the end of each chapter in "Dance of Freedom" section. We will learn to identify life-stealing words and replace them with the life-giving Word of God.

Breakthrough came through the Word

My testimony:

One of the greatest breakthroughs I received was learning Dance of the Word. God was transforming everything about my life through the Word of God. I was a Christian and read my Bible and attended church. I did not understand how to receive the power of the Word. I did not really understand how the Word would transform, heal, and renew.

God used His words to create, bless, curse, build, and destroy. Whatever God spoke came into existence or will come to pass in the future. God magnifies His Word above everything else. He upholds all things by the Word of His power. Everything is upheld by His Word.

By the word of the LORD the heavens were made, and all the host of them by the breath of His mouth. Psa. 33:6

I will worship toward Your holy temple and praise Your name For Your loving kindness and Your truth; For You have magnified Your word above all Your name. Psa. 138:2

God, who at various times and in various ways spoke in time past to the fathers by the prophets, has in these last days spoken to us by His Son, whom He has appointed heir of all things, through whom also He made the worlds; who being the brightness of His glory and the express image of His person, and upholding all things by the Word of His power, when He had by Himself purged our sins, sat down at the right hand of the Majesty on high. Heb 1:1

Speak what God says

Transformation came when I learned to speak the Word of God over myself until I believed what He was saying. Every promise became a treasure. It was not just theological information like before, but it became heart knowledge. Then the power began to work in my heart and life. I began to experience God's power through His Word.

By my confession I was saved. Reading is good, but faith comes by hearing the Word. I cannot hear the Word unless I speak it.

So then faith comes by hearing, and hearing by the Word of God. Rom 10:17

I want to agree with God's Word because it will not return to Him empty. It will accomplish what pleases God, and it will be prosperous or successful. We can be assured that the truth of God never changes. It is reliable, trustworthy, and unwavering.

So shall My word be that goes forth from My mouth; It shall not return to Me void, but it shall accomplish what I please, And it shall prosper in the thing for which I sent it. Is. 55:11

John 1:1–2 tells us that Jesus was Word. He was sent by the Father. Jesus accomplished the purpose for which He sent. Jesus was successful in His role as the sacrificial Lamb and bringing eternal life to all who call upon His name for salvation. He(The Word) returned to the Father accomplishing everything He was supposed to do.

Words are seeds

In nature, a farmer plants and expects to harvest the same seed. He plants carrots and will get a field of carrots. As he sows, he will reap. Our words have the same effect. We reap what we sow over ourselves, relationships, circumstances, or others. Eventually what is sown will become a harvest.

My testimony:

I continually spoke "death" to my self-esteem. I always spoke that I was a victim, codependent, and hopeless and had no worth. I would voice my depression and hopelessness. As I spoke these word seeds into my heart and mind, I became more of what I spoke. I was reaping my harvest. My fear of rejection grew leaps and bounds. I was so desperate for healing. I turned to the Bible and began to speak what God said. Scripture literally became my lifeline and catapulted me into a major overhaul with my self-esteem, worth, and value. This one in particular:

> *Blessed be the God and Father of our Lord Jesus Christ, who has blessed us with every spiritual blessing in the heavenly places in Christ, just as He chose us in Him before the foundation of the world that we should be holy and without blame before Him in love, having predestined us to adoption*

as sons by Jesus Christ to Himself, according to the good
pleasure of His will, to the praise of the glory of His grace,
by which He made us accepted in The Beloved. In Him we
have redemption through His blood, the forgiveness of sins,
according to the riches of His grace. Eph.1:1–7

Accepted? Chosen? Those words were foreign. I had never experienced what they meant. They answered my deepest need. I was accepted. I had worth and value. I decided to start speaking this entire passage daily. I was determined and desperate for healing. I started learning about the power of my words to create and transform. God was teaching me about the power of my words. I became more mindful and intentional of the words I spoke over myself.

Transformation began. My mind became renewed. I began to see the fruit of God's Word in my life. Healing! Deliverance! I was able to leave a nine-year abusive relationship once and for all!

Positive word seeds

Speak word seeds of praise, encouragement, and value over a child, and he will reap a harvest of confidence and healthy self-esteem. This will be an important foundation to all areas of his development, including scholastic, social, and spiritual.

God used positive word seeds when he changed Abram's name to Abraham. In Gen. 17:1–13, God changes Abram's name to Abraham and promises him that he will become the father of many nations. "Abram" means "High Father." "Abraham" means "Father of a Multitude." Every time Abraham hears or speaks his name, he is reminded of God's promises!

God's Word designates His will and promise for our life. When our mind is fixed on God's Word as the governing influence, we become exactly what God says. Abraham's name change shaped his concept of who God says he was. He went from being "High Father" to "Father of a Multitude." That is self-esteem booster! He became exactly what God said.

Negative word seeds

Many of my clients have experienced the awful consequences of negative, harsh, abusive, negligent word seeds that were spoken or implied. Those words created soul wounds, insecurities, and fears and created a negative self-image. There is a childhood rhyme that says, "Sticks and stones will break my bones, but words will never hurt me." Words do hurt. All of us have been hurt by an insult, criticism, or "nickname."

When I was eight, two little boys made a racial slur in "fun." Little did they know how deeply wounded I was. It reinforced my fear of rejection, self-hatred, and low self-esteem. Their words did wound my soul. It would take years before I would learn to love myself. God had to heal so much rejection through His Word. The power of God's love healed my heart.

Power to bind and loose

And I will give you the keys of the kingdom of heaven,
and whatever you bind on earth will be bound in heaven,
and whatever you loose on earth will be loosed in heaven.

Matt.16:19

In this passage, "keys" represent authority. Jesus is giving His church (all believers of Jesus) His authority to control or bind and loose on earth. We can forbid or permit. We use our words to loosen and bind. The same power to bind or loosen is true for the words we speak.

Are your words creating life or death?

Are your words life-giving or life-stealing? Did you know your words have power? The Bible tells us that there is life and death in the power of our tongue. James 3:6 refers to it as fire, a world of iniquity. It can defile the whole body. If our body can be defiled, think what the power of our tongue can do to our life. The Children of Israel spoke negative words resulting in:

- Death to an entire generation
- Wandering for 40 years
- Kept out of the Promised Land
- Kept in a desert

The Children of Israel suffered great consequences because of their untamable tongue. Are you suffering because of your words?

Have they kept you in a desert? Are you reaping word seeds of others or what you have spoken over yourself?

There is life and death in the power of the tongue

Numbers 13–14 demonstrate the power of words. The Children Israel had the opportunity to enter the Promised Land. They chose to believe the "Bad Report" and not believe God's promises.

Because of their "words" a whole generation died in the wilderness. Caleb and Joshua believed and spoke God's promises and entered the Promised Land forty years later. Let us look at the promise given by God before this event.

Promise given

The promise started with Abraham when God promised in Gen. 17:6 that He would make Abraham a great nation and make him exceedingly fruitful and He would make nations out of him and kings will come from Abraham. God will establish his covenant with Abraham's descendants for an everlasting covenant.

This promise was given when the Children of Israel were slaves in Egypt. During hardship and seemingly impossible circumstances God tells them in Exo.3:7 that He has heard their cries and knows their sorrow.

The promise is given more detail when God spoke to Moses in vs.8; He tells them there was a blessed land with lush fertility, unlike the barren desert of Egypt. But there are enemies as well.

The promise is reaffirmed again to Israel while still under bondage in Exo. 6:6

"So I have come down to deliver them out of the hand of the Egyptians, and to bring them up from that land to a good and large land, to a land flowing with milk and honey, to the place of the Canaanites and the Hittites and the Amorites and the Perizzites and the Hivites and the Jebusites." Exo.3:8

"Therefore say to the children of Israel: 'I am the LORD; I will bring you out from under the burdens of the Egyptians, I will rescue you from their bondage, and I will redeem you with an outstretched arm and with great judgments. I will take you as my people, and I will be your God. Then you shall know that I am the LORD your God who brings you out from under the burdens of the Egyptians. And I will bring you into the land which I swore to give to Abraham, Isaac, and Jacob; and I will give it to you as a heritage: I am the LORD." Exo. 6:6

God's power demonstrated in Egypt

In Exodus chapter seven we see the beginning of God's power fulfilling His promise to deliver the Children of Israel. He forewarned Moses that the Pharaoh's heart would be hard, but God will fulfill His Word. During all the plagues, the Children of Israel were miraculously spared. God was making a clear distinction that He was the God of Israel, and no other gods or the king's magicians could equal or surpass Him. Here is a list of the miracles God used to demonstrate His power to Israel and to all of Egypt and to Pharaoh:

- Plague 1: Water becomes blood, 7:14
- Plague 2: frogs, 8:3–15
- Plague 4: flies, 8:20–32
- Plague 5: livestock die. 9:1–12
- Plague 6: Boils, 9:8-12
- Plague 7: Hail, 9:18
- Plague 8: locusts, 10:1-20
- Plague 9: darkness, 10:21-29
- Plague 10: death of the firstborn of man and beast, 11:1–29 (Children of Israel and their firstborn were spared).

God's power demonstrated in the Exodus

- Miracle 1: Pharaoh allows them to leave with their flocks and herds. Exo. 12:31, 32
- Miracle 2: Moses told them to ask the Egyptians for silver, gold, and clothing, and the Egyptians complied and were plundered by the Children of Israel. Exo. 12:35
- Miracle 3: God Himself is leading Israel by a pillar of cloud by day and a pillar of fire by night. Ex, 13:21
- Miracle 4: the Red Sea parted, and instead of mud, there was dry ground to enable them to pass in the middle of

the Red Sea. They passed inbetween walls of water on both sides. Exo. 14:1–22

- Miracle 5: The Red Sea closed back up on the Egyptians, and they were destroyed, including the Pharaoh. Exo. 14: 23–31
- Miracle 6: Bitter waters are turned sweet. Exo.15:22–25
- Miracle 7: God provided manna from heaven every day for forty years. Exo. 16:1–5

Choice to believe God and enter the Promised Land

They were just about to enter the Promised Land. Blessings, abundance, and rich fertile fields promised by the Lord. They had the opportunity to make choices before they entered the Promised Land. In Numbers 13 there were twelve spies who were sent out and found the abundance of produce. It was just as God had promised—a land flowing with milk and honey, and there were enemies. No surprise; God told them in Exo. 3:8 there would be a blessed land, and there would be enemies.

And I am come down to deliver them out of the hand of
the Egyptians, and to bring them up out of that land unto
a good land and a large, unto a land flowing with milk and
honey; unto the place of the Canaanites, and the Hittites, and
the Amorites, and the Perizzites, and the Hivites, and the
Jebusites. Exo. 3:8

Caleb says, "We can!" Ten spies say, "We cannot."

Caleb encouraged them to go up at once and take possession. He remembered God's promises and reminded the other spies. The ten spies said they could not enter the land because of the giants. In Num. 13:32- 33 they gave the Children of Israel a bad report and said, "The land through which we have gone as spies is a land that devours its inhabitants, and all the people whom we saw in it are men of great stature. There we saw the giants (the descendants of Anak came from the giants), and we were like grasshoppers in our own sight, and so we were in their sight."

In Num. 14:3 they continue to speak what they have been saying throughout their exodus. "Why has God brought us to this land to fall by the sword, and all the wives and children become victims? "This was not the first time they thought God or Moses had brought them to die in the wilderness. It happened in Exo. 14:11. In Exo. 17:3, they were thirsty and said that Moses has brought them out of Egypt to kill them, their children, and the livestock with thirst.

Joshua tells them they can take the land because he believes what God had said. He remembers God's promise to defeat their enemies. In Exo.23:20 God promises to send an angel to keep them in their way and bring them in to the Promised Land. He also promises that if they obey His voice, He will be an enemy to their enemies. Joshua has confidence in God's faithfulness and His power. He remembers the miracles and how God defeated the mighty Pharaoh of Egypt.

Behold, I send an Angel before you to keep you in the way and
to bring you into the place which I have prepared. Beware of
Him and obey His voice; do not provoke Him, for He will not
pardon your transgressions; for my name is in Him.

Exo. 23:20

Words kept them out of the Promised Land

In Num. 14: 11–19, God and Moses argue about the fate of Israel.
God wants to kill them because of their continued unbelief. Moses
asks to spare them. Moses states that God does not clear the guilty,
but the iniquity of the fathers passes on to the children to the third
and fourth generation. Because of their murmuring and complain-
ing God said they would not visit the Promised Land. Moses asks
God to pardon their sin (unbelief) according to the greatness of
God's mercy.

God does pardon them but the ones twenty years and older
will die in the wilderness. The number of days they spied the land
(forty) equals the years spent in the wilderness (forty). Caleb and
Joshua were spared because they believed God and agreed and
spoke what He said. They entered the Promised Land forty years
later, just as God had said.

According to their word

In Num. 14:28 God says, "Now tell them this: As surely as I live,
declares the Lord, I will do to you the very things I heard you say"

They stated they would die in the wilderness, and God agreed with them. Because of their choice a whole generation died in the wilderness. Joshua and Caleb entered the Promised Land forty years later because they believed the Lord and chose to speak His promises.

Bad news! Because of their words, an entire generation died in the wilderness. They wandered for forty years in a desert when they could have enjoyed the Promised Land. The good news is that Joshua and Caleb believed and spoke what God said and entered the Promised Land forty years later.

What words are you saying over yourself? Are they life-giving or life-stealing? Have your words kept you in bondage? Are your word seeds reproducing in your life? Are your words mimicking *The Deceiver*'s words or *The Beloved*'s?

God desires that you not just read His Word but understand, believe, and adhere to it as truth. It has the power to change, heal, and restore. He wants you to be rooted deeply and planted by His living water or His Word so that you will be fruitful and strong. He wants you to speak life and not death to yourself and your circumstances.

God's Word is powerful and will accomplish the purpose for which it was sent. Speak the Word and reap His promises, provision, protection, and life-giving power.

God Word is light and life. It has the power to transform, heal, and restore. When His Word is planted within our heart and soul, it will produce fruits of righteousness, peace, love, joy, and healing.

In conclusion, words have great power. They have the power to shape, influence, build, destroy, plant, and bring things into being. We are often the product of words that have been spoken over us. Negative word seeds can produce destruction in our lives.

* * *

Dance with *The Beloved*

Once again, The Beloved offers to dance with Precious. He is the Word. As He speaks truth it feels foreign because all she has heard has been the life-stealing words of The Deceiver. Her wounded heart has so many broken pieces, it seems impossible to comprehend wholeness. The Beloved, relentless in His love, speaks over and over words of life to her broken heart. As she listens and speaks His Word, she sees her heart become new and mended. Life, joy, peace, and love flood the once-darkened places. The dark abyss is now a beautiful well of living water emanating from the Light of The Beloved's glory.

* * *

Dance your way to freedom! Envision yourself as the dancer.
https://mariplanklifecoach.com/dance-of-the-word/

CHAPTER THREE

FOUNDATIONAL STEP #3: DANCE OF LYRICS

The Lord your God in your midst, The Mighty One, will save;
He will rejoice over you with gladness, He will quiet you with
His love, He will rejoice over you with singing. Zeph. 3:17

Love letter from heaven:

Precious One,

My delight is for you to hear My lyrics sung over you. They are songs of love, grace, acceptance, healing, and deliverance. I desire to change what has been sung over you before and replace it with My truth. I desire to transform and restore.

* * *

Precious and The Deceiver are engaged in the Dance of Lyrics. The lyrics are replayed over and over in her heart. The death grip on her heart is unrelenting and suffocating. Negative lyrics swirl in her head, and every time even without thinking about them, she responds with defeat, failure, and discouragement. Old behaviors and attitudes start to surface and become synchronized to the lyrics.

* * *

In the previous chapter we learned the *Dance of the Word*. Words are spoken and unspoken. They may be clear and plainly understood or hidden and masked. They are powerfully conveyed through relationships, events, and circumstances.

The words we speak are like powerful seeds will eventually reap a harvest. The Children of Israel are a somber reminder of the power of our words. They chose to believe and speak the "Bad Report" of *The Deceiver*. A whole generation was kept out of the Promised Land and ended up dying in the wilderness. On the other hand, Joshua and Caleb chose to speak and believe God's Word and were able to enter the Promised Land after the rebellious generation died.

Dance of Word and *Dance of Lyrics* often work together. They play off each other. Remember the goal of *The Deceiver* is to steal, kill, and destroy, according to John 10:10. Similarly, *The Beloved* also uses His Word and lyrics to heal, restore, and set us free.

Why is it a foundational step?

Hundreds of studies have shown that lyrics or words powerfully influence thinking, behavior, and mood, and much of it occurs without conscious awareness. We listen to favorite songs and hum along with them. A commercial with a catchy jingle has us singing along and possibly influences our buying choices. We all have life lyrics that play over and over in our head or heart: "I have to perform," "No one loves me," "There is something wrong with me," "I am always on the outside," "I never fit in," "I have to win," or "I cannot fail."

Life lyrics cause us to respond in certain ways

Researchers have discovered that music and lyrics create "priming." This is when a person is exposed to certain stimuli such as words, lyrics, or surroundings, and their subconscious mind is activated. Once activated, the person's behavior, actions, or attitudes come out in ways that are consistent with the stimulus without awareness of why they are behaving in that manner.

Examples:

My husband (before we were married) and I were driving together, and out of the blue he began to sing, "My baloney has a first name; it is—," and I followed up with "O.S.C.A.R!" I had not heard that commercial in years, yet I was able to quickly recall the tune and words. We were not even discussing food or sandwiches. Why? Because the music and lyrics was in my subconscious, and my husband's singing activated it and without a thought I began to sing along.

The cute images of kids singing about their baloney sandwiches, along with the catchy music and lyrics, had made their way into my brain! When I am shopping and I see that brand, the jingle still plays in my head. I am sure the advertisers love that!

I knew a Vietnam vet who would "hit the deck" or fall on his stomach and cover his head when he heard a car backfire. He was thousands of miles away from a war zone and thirty years later in a San Diego street. Why? The sound triggered an unconscious priming event which caused him to react as if he was still in Vietnam and hearing a gun or bomb blast. "Take cover!" "Hit the Deck!"

Life lyrics or life themes

Advertisers use jingles to market their products and make them memorable and repetitive and hope to influence our choices. *The Deceiver* does the same thing with life lyrics or life themes. one of the common ones I have observed with my clients and most people are as follows:

- Abandonment
- Addictions
- Child abuse
- Control
- Divorce
- Failure

- Insecurity
- Loss
- Powerlessness
- Rejection
- Shame

Life lyrics are repetitive

They are recurring or repetitive in our life and reinforced continuously by *The Deceiver*. Let's look at Pam. She wanted to find validation from men. But she continued to find men who would reject her. Sensing this was a life theme, I began to ask questions, trying to find the source.

Pam's Story:

Before she was born her mom wanted to get an abortion because she couldn't afford another baby. That's rejection from the very beginning of a child's life. Dad left when she was a toddler. Mom remarried, and the stepfather rejected Pam. Rejection continued with every male figure. Her very fear drew the thing she feared the most, rejection.

I mentioned earlier the phenomena of priming with music and lyrics. But this is true for The Deceiver as well. He creates experiences, events, and relationships that begin to create patterns or themes in our life. They are often rooted in our subconscious below our awareness level. Our conscious mind is the things we are aware of and the subconscious stores memories, events, and trauma we have no knowledge of.

Pam had no idea of this pattern of rejection. She did not wake up thinking, "I am going to be rejected today. I will look for someone to reject me." The lyric of rejection planted in her subconscious, and it impacted her behavior, attitudes, and reactions. Her fear of rejection primed her subconscious lyrics of the reality of rejection. Like most of us who have this life lyric, her reaction was 1) to expect rejection and either become needy or clingy to keep the person from leaving, or 2) push the person away to reject them first. The Deceiver wants to reinforce every negative life-stealing lyric.

They are repetitive in nature. They are spoken with the intent of destruction and limitation. It affects our decisions, perceptions, attitudes, behavior, and thinking. Self-perception is shaped and affected by our lyrics. Soul wounds occur. Everything is affected by the life songs we listen to. They become "our truth." What we perceive as "truth" is often reinforced life lyrics.

Life themes or lyrics can be generational. *The Deceiver* often uses families to pass down generational life lyrics to corresponding family members. Pam's ongoing rejection from the men in her life only reinforced her life lyric of rejection. He also passes them down from one generation to another.

Her mom experienced rejection and attracted men who would reject her and her daughter. Pam was driven to fulfill a need for validation. Unfortunately, because of this lyric of rejection, she continued to attract men who would reject her. This repetitive pattern reinforced and strengthened her life lyric.

Family dance

Every family has their own unique "dance." Think of a dance team. Each member plays certain roles. They have their own part of the dance. Each role contributes to the ongoing family dance. When all the members are doing their part there is organized synchronicity. Each member's part in the family dance is determined by many factors. Some of them are given below:

- Abuse
- Communication
- Cultural
- Expectations
- How affection is demonstrated
- Influence of other family members
- Judgments
- Previous lyrics of mother and father and their family
- Relationships
- Unspoken and spoken guidelines, expectations

Within the family dance there are dances between mom and dad, siblings, parent and child, or with other relatives such as aunts, uncles, grandparents, and cousins. All of these contribute to *Dance of Lyrics*. Some may be good, and others may become dysfunctional, giving *The Deceiver* power to create destruction and limitation.

Examples from my family:

- *My grandma was a victim of domestic violence and so was I*
- *Divorce was rampant in my family*
  - *Mom and Dad divorced*
  - *Mom remarried and divorced*
  - *My brother divorced his first wife; remarried her and she divorced him again*
  - *My husband's parents were divorced*
  - *My husband was divorced by his first wife*
  - *I was divorced*
  - *My son was divorced twice*
  - *My daughter is filing for divorce*
  - *My niece was divorced*

Other common generational lyrics:

- Men who had controlling moms marry controlling women.
- Child abuse victims will often marry child abusers or allow abusers to have access to their children.
- Children of alcoholics will marry an alcoholic or another child of an alcoholic.

Family lyrics can be good and life-giving or bad and life-stealing. Many are benign or neutral and don't affect our life lyrics as much. Some lyrics may be good, but *The Deceiver* will pollute and twist them into something life-stealing. The Holy Spirit can help you untwist the ones that have been distorted. He can replace the bad ones with His lyrics. He will sing over you His lyrics of grace and redemption.

My testimony:

One of the unspoken lyrics in my family was "honor." It was never defined. We all knew it was something to always work for. We were to honor our family by doing well in school, etc. Honor is defined as moral integrity, credibility, or right standing. Honor is good. But for me it became destructive because the enemy polluted the purity of this word by making me think that honor equaled performance. Performance equaled acceptance. So, to feel accepted I had to perform.

Example:

Sylvia had a protective father. She was dependent totally on her father for everything. Being a protective father is good. Providing for all her needs is important. At eighteen she was kicked out of her house. After all she was an adult, and it was time to leave the nest. Because of her dad's overprotectiveness, she never learned how to make choices or be independent. She lacked confidence in herself and didn't know how to protect herself. One hour after she was kicked out, she turned to prostitution. I imagine that one of her life lyrics was child sexual abuse.

Sadly, somewhere a lyric was planted in her soul that performing sexually was a way to get protection and provision. The

Deceiver polluted and twisted her lyrics. Sylvia had a multitude of twisted lyrics causing her so much pain and heartache.

We see from these previous examples how some life lyrics can develop from things not intentionally evil such as honor, protectiveness, and provision. *The Deceiver* twists the lyrics and adds bad or destructive lyrics and pollutes our soul even more. We also see *The Deceiver*'s intentional planting of damaging lyrics in our lives. His lies or lyrics are planted deep in our subconscious, waiting for the moment when "priming occurs" and the lyrics are brought to our conscious mind. The more we allow those lies to direct our actions, attitudes, or emotions, the more they are reinforced.

These family dances can be ways *The Deceiver* transmits his lyrics over our life. Because they are repetitive in nature, they are driven deep into our soul and subconscious, waiting for the moment to be awakened. Once the lyrics are awakened, they are reinforced and destruction is driven deeper into our life. All we know are the lyrics we listen to. They become our reality or our "truth." Just like a tree, the natural progression is the production of fruit which bears seed. Seed is thrown into our soil, and it either nourishes the tree or creates another tree.

What is truth?

It is our reality, actuality, certainty, or law. We accept *The Deceiver*'s lyrics as true, correct, accurate, right, faithful, and factual. In Pam's case, rejection was her "truth." It was a reality. It was reinforced by fact-based proof. Her life experiences reinforced that it was true.

We can start accepting and speaking God's Word as our truth. The same process we saw earlier will occur. His Word nourishes our soil and our thoughts are renewed and we produce His fruit. God's Word is the only truth, and it will set us free.

And you shall know the truth, and the truth shall make you free. John 8:32

Jesus is the way, truth, and life. Jesus said to him, "I am the way, the truth, and the life. No one comes to the Father except through Me." John 14:6

The Holy Spirit guides us into all truth. However, when He, the Spirit of truth, has come, He will guide you into all truth; for He will not speak on His own authority, but whatever He hears He will speak; and He will tell you things to come.
John 16:13

God's Truth vs. *The Deceiver's* Lies

God's Truth	The Deceiver's Lies
Restores, delivers	Limitation, destruction
Is plainly written and not hidden; it is known	Are hidden, masked, and often unknown
Is always motivated by God's love	Is always motivated by *The Deceiver's* hatred toward anything good

Will heal	Will wound
Sets us free	Creates bondage

My testimony:

I have a similar testimony to Pam's. One of my life lyrics was also fear of rejection. It did not come from abusive parents. It did not come from my mom wanting an abortion. It simply came from my parents unable to meet my emotional needs. They meant well. But in our culture, it was not accepted or promoted to affirm your children. I never received hugs for validation. I knew intellectually they loved me, but I never felt it. I grew up in an emotionally sterile environment.

Adding cultural performance issues to the lack of love created a destructive series of life lyrics. I perceived that the only way to avoid rejection was to perform. So, performance became my HUGE way to avoid the fear of rejection and find love. Of course, being needy made me codependent. This caused me to "find" someone as dysfunctional and needy as I was. Unfortunately, the generational life lyric of domestic violence skipped my mom and dad and landed on me. I was attracted to someone who was abusive, just like my grandma.

Like Pam, I sought out men who would reject me, which led to my abusive husband. Abuse only reinforced my fear of rejection. I reached a critical point in my life where I either needed to believe and seek after what God said or continue to listen to The Deceiver. Through the course of time I listened to God's Word. My old lyrics became God's Word. He is singing songs of love and healing over me.

Your decrees have been the theme of my songs wherever I have lived. Ps. 119:54 (New Living Translation)

You are my hiding place; you shall preserve me from trouble; you shall surround me with songs of deliverance.
Selah Psalm 32:7

In conclusion, in order to *Stop Dancing with the Enemy*, we need to identify life lyrics or lies that are life-stealing and replace them with the life-giving truth of God's Word. *The Deceiver* wants to "prime" our lyrics with his lies of destruction. He wants us to activate them through believing and acting as if they are true. *The Beloved* wants us to believe His truth and experience the fullness of grace, redemption, and transformation.

* * *

Dance with *The Beloved*

Once again, *The Beloved* offers to dance with Precious. He is the Word. As He speaks truth it feels foreign because all she has heard has been the life-stealing words of *The Deceiver*. Her wounded heart has so many broken pieces, it seems impossible to comprehend wholeness. *The Beloved*, relentless in His love, speaks over and over words of life to her broken heart. As she listens and speaks His Word, she sees her heart become new and mended. Life, joy, peace, and love flood the once-darkened places. The dark abyss is now a beautiful well of living water emanating from the Light of *The Beloved's* glory.

* * *

Dance your way to freedom! Envision yourself as the dancer. https://mariplanklifecoach.com/dance-of-lyrics/

CHAPTER FOUR

FOUNDATIONAL STEP 4: DANCE OF FORGIVENESS

Bear with each other and forgive one another if any of you has a grievance against someone. Forgive as the Lord forgave you. Col. 3:13 NIV

Love letter from heaven:

Precious One,

How I long for you to understand how important this foundational step is for your total healing. Unforgiveness has kept you in prison, in darkness, and it has given The Deceiver the right and authority to torment you. I know forgiveness is difficult and almost impossible. But as you choose to forgive, I will set your heart and soul free.

* * *

The Deceiver and Precious are dancing. She sees images and memories of all the people who hurt, betrayed, offended, or abused her. Deep tormenting pain and anguish knife through her heart, filleting the very depths of her soul. "That person doesn't deserve your forgiveness. Look what they did! He deserves punishment or retaliation."

The Deceiver continues to remind her of the injustices done to her. Oozing from her heart was the thick, tar-like black liquid. The stench was indescribable, putrid, and nauseating. They wrap around her like unrelenting tentacles. Her unforgiveness is all-consuming. The tentacles wrap themselves throughout her heart. Barb-like teeth grip every part of her heart and soul. The tentacles extend from her heart right into the hands of The Deceiver. They resemble a puppeteer who controls the puppet thorough the attached wires.

* * *

Why is this a foundational step?

Definition: forgiveness is the setting of one's will, the making of a decision (a decree, a decision at the spiritual level). A release is granted to the offender. To pardon.

Forgiveness of self and others is essential to learning how to dance with *The Beloved*. Unforgiveness impacts our spiritual, physical, and emotional health. It keeps us in prison and subject to being tormented by *The Deceiver*.

My testimony:

This was me. I had so much unforgiveness, bitterness, anger, and resentment in my heart. It was eating me up. I was like a puppet being controlled by The Deceiver. He was causing me to continually think about the pain and injustice. He used it to provoke rage and anger inside. At one point I wanted to hurt my husband.

I decided to forgive. It was not easy. It was a hard process but well worth it. It took a while, but eventually the rage and anger were gone. The black stench of bitterness has been washed away by The Beloved's grace and mercy. The Deceiver does not have his tentacles wrapping around me, nor does he control my emotions or actions.

Before, I could think about my abuse and experience the pain and rage as if I were still being abused. Now when I tell my story, there is no pain! I can relive the moment but am detached from the agony. It is like watching a movie. I see the violent-filled relationship playing out on the screen, but I do not feel the pain. Only the love and power of Jesus could take away my pain.

Consequences of unforgiveness

Unforgiveness creates soul wounds. Our spirit is instantly renewed when we are born again, but our soul carries wounds, memories, offenses, and our sinful nature. Unforgiveness gives the enemy legal access or a landing place in our soul. He is a source and cause of these wounds to steal, kill, and destroy, but Jesus has come to give us abundant life. The greatest source of soul wounds is unforgiveness.

Unforgiveness gives *The Deceiver* the right to torment. In Matthew 18: 21–35 we are told of one man who owed money equivalent to sixteen years of wages to his master. He went to the master to whom the money was owed. The master was going to sell him and his family and all he had, but the man asked for mercy.

The master had compassion and was forgiven of his debt. The same man went to someone who owed him money equivalent to one day's wages. And he demanded what was owed. His debtor asked for mercy but was denied and was thrown into prison.

The master heard what had happened and said because the man did not show mercy and compassion to the one who owed him one day's wages, he would be turned over to the tormentor in (verses 32–35). Torment is extreme pain or anguish.

For the enemy has pursued and persecuted in my soul, he has crushed my life down to the ground. He has made me dwell in dark places as those who have been long dead. Ps.143:3

We set up monuments for the offense. We remember what wrong occurred and are tormented by *The Deceiver*. In Mark 5:1–20 there was demonized man who lived among the tombs. They are monuments or places to remember the deceased. We set up monuments for the offense and remember what wrong occurred. If there is unforgiveness, we will be tormented by *The Deceiver*. Jesus healed the demonized man, and he was restored in his right mind and no longer lived among the tombs.

Unforgiveness causes us torment. Torment means to cause trouble, disturb, harass, cause mental affliction, difficulty, and it defiles us. This is what unforgiveness will do to us. We become corrupt and polluted according to Heb. 12:15.

See to it that no one falls short of the grace of God and that no bitter root grows up to cause trouble and defile many.
Heb. 12:15, NIV

It can cause illness. "When harbored for a long time," says Professor Wrosch, "bitterness may forecast patterns of biological deregulation (a physiological impairment that can affect metabolic immune response or organ function) and physical disease." Ian Fletcher says, "Harboring feelings of bitterness increases the likelihood of physical disease,"www.dailymail.co.uk/health/article-2024386/ Harbouring-bitterness-increases-likelihood-physical-disease.html

For I see that you are poisoned by bitterness and bound by iniquity. Acts 8:23

It is sin. In Romans 1:18–32, Paul talks about the wrath of God against unrighteousness. His righteous and personal anger is against all sin. Rather than to bring Him honor, sin dishonors Him and contradicts His holy and moral character. Paul's list of sins is detailed. Unforgiveness is on this list of sins.

For the wrath of God is revealed from heaven against all ungodliness and unrighteousness of men, who suppress the truth in unrighteousness because what may be known of God

*is manifest in them, for God has shown it to them. For since
the creation of the world His invisible attributes are clearly
seen, being understood by the things that are made, even His
eternal power and Godhead, so that they are without excuse,
because, although they knew God, they did not glorify Him as
God, nor were thankful, but became futile in their thoughts,
and their foolish hearts were darkened. Professing to be wise,
they became fools, and changed the glory of the incorruptible
God into an image made like corruptible man—and birds
and four-footed animals and creeping things. Therefore God
also gave them up to uncleanness, in the lusts of their hearts,
to dishonor their bodies among themselves, who exchanged
the truth of God for the lie, and worshiped and served the
creature rather than the Creator, who is blessed forever.
Amen. For this reason, God gave them up to vile passions.
For even their women exchanged the natural use for what is
against nature. Likewise, also the men, leaving the natural
use of the woman, burned in their lust for one another, men
with men committing what is shameful, and receiving in
themselves the penalty of their error which was due. And
even as they did not like to retain God in their knowledge,
God gave them over to a debased mind, to do those things
which are not fitting; being filled with all unrighteousness,
sexual immorality, wickedness, covetousness, maliciousness;
full of envy, murder, strife, deceit, evilmindedness; they are
whisperers, backbiters, haters of God, violent, proud, boasters,*

inventors of evil things, disobedient to parents, undiscerning,
*untrustworthy, unloving, **UNFORGIVING**, unmerciful;*
who, knowing the righteous judgment of God, that those who
practice them.
Rom. 1:18–32

Are you surprised that unforgiveness is listed with such sins
as murder, adultery, sexual immorality? As a new believer when
I first read this, I was surprised and thought unforgiveness was a
"lesser" sin. Sin is sin in God's eyes.

It keeps God from forgiving us. I don't know about you, but I
need God's forgiveness every minute of every day. I make mistakes,
miss the mark, sin, and stray from His paths of righteousness. I
don't want to hinder His forgiveness with my unforgiveness.

For if you forgive men their trespasses, your heavenly Father
will also forgive you. But if you do not forgive men their
trespasses, neither will your Father forgive your trespasses.
Matt. 6: 14, 15

Forgiveness transforms

I would like to share some poignant testimonies about the power of
forgiveness. Some of the testimonies are from my clients, friends,
and the stories of others. All of them start out with people who are
being tormented, limited, stopped, or defeated. They all end with

glorious deliverance and healing and were all done through the power of Jesus.

Note: some of the things that were forgiven are not necessarily known offenses. Nevertheless, forgiveness was applied, and freedom occurred.

Forgiveness unlocked God-given passion for art. Joan's art was mechanical and lacked passion. Her father told her that her art would never make any money. So, she pursued a career in interior office design. It was dry and mechanical. She forgave her father and after her coaching, her art became wild, crazy, and passionate. She took back her God-given artistic ability. Now she has an art gallery! Forgiveness unlocked her God-given passion for art.

Forgiveness healed a twenty-year struggle! Mark looked at a book and saw colors and numbers rather than words. He suffered for twenty years and sought medical and psychiatric help. He was molested by a Catholic priest when he was three. It makes sense that a three-year-old who sees things in colors and numbers would try and cover up what had happened with colors and numbers. After he forgave the priest, he took back his right as a child of God to have soundness of mind He was healed and able to see the words instead of colors! Forgiveness healed a twenty-year struggle!

Forgiveness healed her from pain! Anna asked for prayer because she was experiencing pain that would travel throughout her body. The Lord told me, "witchcraft.". Anna's parents were involved in witchcraft, but she was not. I told her that sometimes when ancestors are involved in witchcraft it could cause physical pain or torment. I asked her to forgive her parents for being involved in witchcraft. She forgave them and used the blood of Jesus to cover any other wounds it may have caused. Instantly the pain left. Forgiveness healed her from pain!

Forgiveness was the key to freedom. *Alice, an African American, was perpetually late. She was at peace if she was ten to fifteen minutes late. Anxiety and fear flooded her heart if she was on time. Usually it is the opposite, and people are anxious when they are late. I asked her what she believed about being on time. She was told by relatives that being on time meant you were on time for a lynching or hanging. (This was a terrible reality for many African Americans).*

By being late, she would avoid something bad. That is why she was more at peace when she arrived later. I told her that as a professional she could not keep doing this and keep people waiting. It would give her a bad reputation and possibly ruin important and much needed connections.

I suggested that she forgive her relatives for telling her this lie and take back the right to be on time. She did, and amazingly, she was able to arrive early or on time and was free of the anxiety and fear that used to accompany her. The Deceiver had been tormenting her all this time.

Vindication and punishment are God's responsibility

My testimony:

Forgiving my ex-husband was one of the hardest things I had to do. There were so many years of abuse, heartache, trauma, and victimization. My heart was so filled with anger, resentment, and bitterness. I knew I had to learn how to forgive. Vindication and punishment are God's responsibility, not mine.

I made the decision to forgive Fred. It was not because he earned or deserved it. I knew that it was right before the Lord. I forgave Fred at least a hundred times a day. Well, it seemed like it was that many. Choosing to forgive caused the well of pain, anger, and resentment to become less and less. I reached a point where there was no more anger in my heart. God doesn't ask us to forget but to forgive.

Have you ever said, "That person really makes me angry?" The person cannot make us do anything. We choose to be angry, resentful, and bitter. I know people carry grudges and unforgiveness for twenty years. They are miserable, unhappy, and often physically sick.

Scriptures:

- Forgive those who offend us. Mk. 11:25–26, Matt. 6:14–15, Matt. 18:15–17
- Offer forgiveness to someone we have offended. Matt. 5:23–24

- Forgiveness comes from the heart. Mat. 18:35
- Forgive as much as necessary until your heart is clean. Matt. 18:21–22
- Forgive and be cleansed. I John 1:9

The misconceptions of forgiveness

- Forgiveness does not justify the offense or offender.
- Forgiveness is not determined by my feelings.
- Forgiveness is not determined by the worthiness of the offender.
- Forgiveness is not always a one-time event; it is a process.

Who do I need to forgive?

- Anyone who has hurt or offended you.
- Anyone who has caused you limitations, captivity. Remember our examples of Joan, Pam, Alice, and Mark?
- Myself. There is no condemnation for those in Christ Jesus. See Rom. 8:1
- My ancestors for passing down generational sin, addictions, behaviors, beliefs, attitudes, etc.

How do I forgive?

- Decide it is not based upon feelings.
- Continue to forgive until the pain is gone.
- Ask the Holy Spirit to help you.

In conclusion, forgiveness of self and others is essential to learning how to dance with *The Beloved*. Unforgiveness impacts our spiritual, physical, and emotional health. It keeps us in prison and subject to being tormented by *The Deceiver*. There are spiritual, emotional, and physical consequences to unforgiveness.

* * *

Dance with *The Beloved*

Precious and The Beloved began the Dance of Freedom. Precious con- fesses her bitterness and anger toward those who hurt her. She for- gives anyone who created an emotional or spiritual limitation. Every time she forgave the thick, tar-like black liquid began to change color. Even though the stench was indescribable, putrid, and nauseating, The Beloved was not offended by the odor, but gladly took it from her. Before, unforgiveness wrapped around her like unrelenting tentacles. But now, it was losing its death grip. Bitterness no longer consumed her heart. The most amazing thing happened! Previous memories which tormented her no longer had the power to make her respond as before. She saw The Beloved take a mighty sword and severe the marionette wires once used by The Deceiver to control and influence Precious. Her soul was now free!

* * *

Dance your way to freedom! Envision yourself as the dancer. https://mariplanklifecoach.com/dance-of-forgiveness/

CHAPTER FIVE

DANCE OF RIGHTEOUSNESS: OVERCOMING SHAME

I will greatly rejoice in the Lord, my soul shall be joyful in my

God. For He has clothed me with the garments of salvation,

He has covered me with the robe of righteousness, as a

bridegroom decks himself with ornaments, and as a bride

adorns herself with her jewels. Isa. 61:10

Love letter from heaven:

Precious One,

How I long for you to overcome and know the redemptive work of My Son, Jesus, on the cross. He bore your shame, guilt, and sin. I have covered you with His robes of righteousness. Your shame, guilt, and sin have been made white as snow.

* * *

Precious looks down and sees the filthy, disgusting garments she is wearing. They remind her of how she feels inside. She feels "dirty," "flawed," and beyond redemption. The Deceiver begins the dance. Her filthiness makes her unlovable and unwanted. He whispers in her ear, "You are damaged goods." "Why would anyone love you?" "You deserved what happened to you." "It was all your fault." He knows the power of shame and intentionally plants it in her root system and continues to reinforce shame. The Deceiver is quick to point out every flaw. They are magnified in Precious's eyes.

* * *

What is shame?

Shame's message is, "I am bad," or "There is something wrong with me." It is a painful feeling of humiliation or distress caused by the awareness that you are "flawed," "dirty," or "unclean." It comes from fear accompanied with feelings of unworthiness and unlovable. It is a pervasive feeling that never goes away.

What does shame look like?

- It can be hidden, so we are often unaware that we have shame.
- When we experience shame, it lasts much longer than momentary embarrassment or humiliation.

- The feelings and pain associated with shame are of greater intensity.
- An external event isn't required to trigger it. Our own thoughts can bring on feelings of shame.
- It can lead to spirals of depression and feelings of hopelessness and despair.
- *The Deceiver* will often use messages, images, or beliefs originating in childhood and paint a negative "shame story" about ourselves.
- It creates deep feelings of inadequacy.

Where does shame come from?

Within every family we have lyrics or beliefs or "rules" that govern everything within the family. Relationships, communication, conflict resolution, emotional and physical intimacy, interaction with the outside world are all orchestrated by the "family rules." These rules act like walls that are rigid or flexible.

Family dysfunction is on a continuum of healthy and unhealthy. There are no "perfect" families. The level of dysfunction will affect the emotional and social development of every member. This is where we learn most of our dances. It is often where *The Deceiver* creates and reinforces our negative lyrics or belief systems.

Family rules

A family "rule" is something known or unknown that dictates how a family behaves, handles conflict, communicates, and expresses feelings or opinions. They define the structure of the family and relationships within the family. Rules often can have serious and detrimental effects on a child. An example of a "rule" is, "Children should be seen and not heard." This rule diminishes the child's very existence. It gives the clear message that the child is invisible and doesn't matter. This would inflict a sense of worthlessness in a child.

Healthy families have rules, but they are flexible and can be adapted to change. It allows new information brought to the family and the ability to adapt to a new "normal." Members feel respected, loved, and free to communicate opinions and emotions.

There are healthy boundaries within the relationships or subsets. A subset is mom and dad, mom and sister, sister and brother, father and sister, father and brother, etc. Each boundary around the subset and around the family is healthy, flexible, and adaptable.

Rules that govern shame-based families:

Control. One must be in control of all interactions, feelings, and personal behavior at all times. (Control is the major defense strategy for shame.)

Perfectionism. Always be right in everything you do. (Family members live according to an externalized image. No one ever measures up.)

Blame. Whenever things don't turn out as planned, blame yourself or others. (Blame is another cover-up for shame.)

Denial of the five freedoms. You should not perceive, think, feel, desire, or imagine the way you do. (You should do these the way the perfectionist ideal demands.)

The No-Talk Rule. I cannot express my feelings, needs, or wants.

Don't Make Mistakes. If you admit a mistake, it will reveal how flawed or vulnerable you are. Cover up your mistakes, and if someone else makes a mistake, shame them. (To acknowledge a mistake is to open oneself to scrutiny.)

Unreliability. Don't trust anyone, and you will never be disappointed. (The parents did not get their developmental dependency needs met and will not be there for their children to depend on.) https://www.wasatchfamilytherapy.com/archives/27781

How does shame impact a family?

Shame enters from significant people in our lives and becomes a part of our root system. It nourishes the trunk or lyrics and results in the fruit of shame and its various expressions. Members within a shame-driven family will display various indications of shame. Some are more obvious, and some remain hidden. Shame is woven into the tapestry of rules, lyrics, emotions, and relationships.

Shame becomes pervasive or chronic through intense experiences of shame in childhood. Parents can unintentionally transfer their shame to their children through verbal messages or nonverbal behavior. For an example, a child might feel unloved in reaction to a parent's depression, indifference, absence, or irritability. They may feel inadequate due to a parent's competitiveness or over-correcting behavior, criticism, condemnation, or comparing to others.

Chronic or pervasive shame can lead to aggression, depression, eating disorders, PTSD, and addictions. It generates low self-esteem, anxiety, irrational guilt, perfectionism, and codependency. It limits our ability to enjoy satisfying relationships and professional success. It creates deep wells of pain and suffering. It becomes an integral part of our dance with *The Deceiver*.

Shame usually enters in childhood through the following:

Physical or emotional abandonment. This creates insecurity, fear of abandonment, or rejection.

Rejection and unmet needs. This could be directly or indirectly through parents' illness, busyness, or preoccupation with other problems. They are unable to meet a child's emotional needs for love, acceptance, and approval.

Labels, name calling. Ridicule reinforces a child's lyrics that she or he is "flawed," "less than," or not enough.

Keeping "secrets." Most abusive families maintain their dysfunction by "keeping secrets." Family members are required to stay silent to protect the family. Parental disbelief, defending the abuser, or accusations will shame the child into silence, denial, pretending, or acting out. Disclosure and getting help are seen as bad and a threat to the family.

My testimony:

As a child my shame did not come from an overtly dysfunctional family. It came from my sense of inadequacy and not measuring up. My parents never criticized or condemned me. They never validated my feelings or told me I was loved. The unintentional message I received was, "I was not enough" or "There was something wrong with me." Before my healing journey began, shame was a rampant part of my pain and distress. It exacerbated victimization, low selfesteem, insecurity, fear, codependency, hopelessness, and helplessness. They all work together. They play off each other and reinforce each other as well.

I was ashamed because I was a Christian and dated a non-Christian. Not only did I date a non-Christian, but I got pregnant and had an abortion at sixteen, got pregnant again, and end up marrying him. My domestic abuse made me feel ashamed, flawed, messed up, and hopeless. It promoted bouts of depression, anxiety, and fear.

I was ashamed because of all of the number of times (nine in total) that I left Fred, involving friends and family and running away, and how it impacted my children. I was ashamed because I couldn't get out of the cycle of abuse and kept returning over and over again to an abusive situation. Every time I reached out for help, and every time I returned it increased my sense of shame.

I was ashamed that I had to go on welfare because Fred was not supporting the kids. Back then, recipients of welfare would separate their groceries from non-eligible and eligible food items when you're at the grocery checkout line. And then, you had to hand her the food stamps to pay for the groceries. The stares of "judgment" I felt in the back of my head from people behind me went straight to my core of shame.

Dance of Righteousness

What is righteousness? Righteousness (dikaisune in Greek) means just, the quality of being right. God declares a believer righteous, the sense of acquitting him, and imparts righteousness to him.

The Dance of Righteousness is not only a critical component to overcoming shame, but it is a main ingredient as we dance with *The Beloved.* We need to lay hold, apprehend, or appropriate the redemptive work of Jesus on the cross. The work of the cross is deep, profound, complete, healing, and restorative.

Imagine the owner of your favorite store gives you 24/7 access to his store. Everything in the store is free. Anything and everything you could possibly imagine is yours. The owner gives you one condition: you must take what you want out of the store.

Every day you sit outside the store thinking about all the things you want, need, and long for. You can peer through the door and windows and can see everything your heart desires inside the store.

Until you follow the owner's directions. You'll never be able to own the very thing you want.

This is a picture of us as believers not taking hold or appropriating the work of the cross. A more appropriate picture would be that of a king who opens the doors of his vast, limitless treasury and tells you that everything you need for life, godliness, healing, restoration, and transformation is available. You just need to make it yours. We make it ours when we take these precious promises and speak, claim, and believe. This will eradicate shame.

Paul tells us:

> *"Not that I have already attained, or am already perfected, but I press on, that I may lay hold of that for which Christ Jesus has already laid hold of me."* Phil. 3:12

What can we appropriate at the cross regarding shame?

Our faith in Jesus made us righteous. For what does the scripture say? "Abraham believed God, and it was accounted to him for righteousness." Rom. 4:3 The Greek word for account is logidzomai; it means to numerically to count, compute, and sum up and to consider, reckon, reason, deem, evaluate, or value. Logidzomai finalizes thought, judges' matter, draws logical conclusions, decides outcomes, and puts every action into a debit or credit position.

This means that God added up, calculated all our sin, shame, insecurities, fears, etc. which equaled a huge insurmountable debt. He evaluated, reasoned, deemed, and judged our faith in Christ and came to a logical conclusion and put His righteousness as a credit to our account! Essentially, He said our debt of sin was paid in full by Jesus.

Think of the magnitude of this! As far as God is concerned, the shame we bear is now covered by His righteousness. God only sees us through the blood of Jesus. Not only was our debt wiped out, so our accounts were paid, but then God gave us a huge "credit." Jesus's righteousness was an incredible asset!

We are outfitted with the Robe of Righteousness. *I will sing for joy in God, explode in praise from deep in my soul! He dressed me up in a suit of salvation; he outfitted me in a robe of righteousness, as a bridegroom who puts on a tuxedo and a bride a jeweled tiara. For as the earth bursts with spring wildflowers, and as a garden cascades with blossoms, so the Master, God, brings righteousness into full bloom and puts praise on display before the nations.* Isaiah 61:10 The Msg. Bible

We are the righteousness of God in Him. *For He made Him who knew no sin to be sin for us, that we might become the righteousness of God in Him.* 2 Cor. 5:21

We are cleansed or pure as snow. What is pure? It is free of any contamination. *"Come now, and let us reason together,"* Says the Lord, *"Though your sins are like scarlet, they shall be as white as*

snow; though they are red like crimson, they shall be as wool." Isaiah 1:18 NKJV

This is huge for shame-bound people, especially victims of abuse. Often victims of sexual abuse feel "dirty" or "unclean" or "used goods." God says you are white as the driven snow. His love and Word can wash all the filth and dirt of our soul and heart. This includes shame.

Not flawed but a masterpiece. You are a masterpiece created in Christ Jesus. For we are God's masterpiece. He has created us anew in Christ Jesus, so we can do the good things He planned for us long ago. Eph 2:10, NLT

What is condemnation?

It means to declare to be reprehensible, wrong, or evil usually after weighing evidence and without reservation. Condemnation is the voice of *The Deceiver* bringing judgment, accusation, and declaration of how repulsive, bad, or flawed we are. It feeds on our shame, insecurity, fears, and self-loathing. Everything that is negative, wrong, and imperfect becomes the target of condemnation.

We see Paul's view of condemnation in Romans 7. He is acknowledging the struggle with his sinful nature and the new man which is regenerated through Jesus. Paul says the good he wants to do, he doesn't do. The evil he doesn't want to do, he does. He sees himself as wretched (miserable, unhappy, sad, contemptible, and despicable). It sounds like shame has gotten a hold of Paul.

But in the next chapter, he realizes there is no condemnation for anyone in Christ. He is confident of his new position in Christ. Despite the war we face between our sinful nature and the new man, we are not under God's judgment. This internal war doesn't change God's view of us! Again, He sees us in Christ and in His righteousness.

So now there is no condemnation for those who belong to Christ Jesus. Rom. 8:1 NLT

My testimony:

During my healing journey, I was pregnant with my third child. Following my history of leaving Fred and coming back, I found myself in the same situation I had been two times before. I was planning to tell my dad when I heard the voice of the The Deceiver. "Look, you are pregnant again, what is your dad going to say?" It was dripping with condemnation. I was becoming strong in the Lord and learning to wield the Sword of The Spirit (the Word of God) effectively against The Deceiver and his lies.

Without even thinking about it, I held up my hand like a police officer stopping traffic and yelled, "Shut up." He and I knew what that meant. There was no condemnation because I was in Christ Jesus. I imagined he was choking on his words. It became incredibly quiet, and I never heard that accusation again!

In conclusion, shame often comes from our family roots through relationships or experiences. It causes us to feel "less than," "flawed," "dirty," "not enough." It can result in depression and low self-esteem and will cause us to recreate shame in our lives.

We can overcome shame by appropriating Jesus's death and resurrection. We need to accept His Robe of Righteousness and truth that our shame was nailed to the cross. In God's eyes, He sees us through the precious blood of Jesus. He says we are redeemed and pure.

Dance of Freedom

Let's take the four foundational steps and apply them to the *Dance of Righteousness*; each step is important to the entire *Dance of Freedom*. Take some time to pray and ask the Holy Spirit to help you and reveal truth. God's truth will set you free.

And you shall know the truth, and the truth shall make you free. John 8:32

Let's review the definition of righteousness: (dikaiosume in Greek) just, the quality of being right. Broadly, the word suggests conformity to the revealed will of God in all respect. Righteousness is both judicial (pertaining to justice) and gracious. God declares the believer righteous by acquitting him and imparting righteousness through Jesus.

Foundational Step #1: Dance of Awareness

The Dance of Awareness is important because it helps us to understand the relationship between our fruit (attitudes, actions, emotions), our trunk (beliefs or lyrics), and our soil (relationships, events, circumstances).

Fruit: Circle the fruit on your tree:

- Childhood abuse
- Depression
- Eating disorders
- Fear of rejection
- Feel insignificant
- Feel small
- Feel unworthy
- Feeling dirty or unclean
- Hopelessness
- Inadequacy
- Plagued with fears
- Poor boundaries
- Shame

Prayer:

Father,

You see my fruit of shame. Help me when I feel inadequate, dirty, depressed, hopeless, or fearful. You have covered me with the

Robe of Righteousness given to me through my acceptance of Jesus. You see me without blemish or flaws. I am pure as snow. Holy Spirit, You are the power that raised Christ from the dead, and You dwell in me. Help me to believe You see me as righteous.

How shame affects our roots or soil

As shame is passed through our family tree it makes its way into our soil or roots. It weaves itself in and through our childhood with reinforced messages like "I am flawed or damaged." Experiences of failure, rejection, physical or emotional abandonment, or child abuse can create shame.

What sources of shame are in your roots or soil? Circle all that apply:

- Abandonment
- Abuse
- Control
- Denial of feelings
- Family secrets
- Feeling dirty or unclean
- No talk rules
- perfectionism
- Poor boundaries
- Rejection
- Unreliability

Prayer:

Father,

You see my roots of shame. Holy Spirit, I know You cannot change my past, but You can change how it affected me. Pour out Your power and love in my root system. Saturate every area of shame with Your perfect love and Word.

Thank You. I am pure and a new creature in Christ. You bore my shame and rejection. I give You these roots and ask for Your healing and the precious blood of Jesus over them. I desire to be a tree planted by Your Living Water. Nourished, and strengthened. Let Your redemptive work secured by Jesus's death and resurrection manifest in my roots.

Foundational Step #2: Dance of the Word

Words have great power. They have the power to shape, influence, build, destroy, plant, and bring things into life. Think of the words you have heard. It doesn't matter if they came from people, *The Deceiver*, or yourself. You were influenced and affected by their power. Circle the words of shame have heard

- You are a failure
- You are bad
- You are dirty
- You are flawed
- You are inadequate
- You are insignificant

- You are mistake
- You are rejection
- You are small
- You are unlovable

Write down other ones:

_____

_____

_____

Prayer:

Father,

You see the words of shame that have impacted me. You know the destruction it has caused. Forgive me for listening to them. Help me to cling to Your Word. Holy Spirit, give me a desire and passion to speak Your Word over and over until it produces the fruit of righteousness within.

Consider what happened to Lazarus in John 11. He was lifeless and dead for four days before Jesus arrived. His body was decaying. Jesus (the Word) came because He loved Martha, Mary, and their brother, and He wanted to show them God's glory. He approached the tomb and called out, "Lazarus, come forth." Lazarus did exactly what the Word said and came out of the tomb, still wearing the grave clothes he was wrapped in.

God's Word went forth, and the Holy Spirit began to activate Lazarus's physical functioning. Lazarus's brain began to activate, causing all his organs and systems to function! Lungs filled with air and began breathing. Blood circulated and life flowed again through his once-dead body!

Hear *The Beloved* say, "_____ (your name), come out of the tomb of shame."

"Come back to life from shame."

"Death and decay can no longer hold you."

Speak God's resurrection power over your life. When *The Deceiver* tries to make you feel shame, take authority over it and be aggressive with the Word of God. Don't let him lure you back into the tomb of shame. Jesus has come to bring you His resurrection power and deliver you from the tomb of shame.

Jesus said to her, "I am the resurrection and the life. He who believes in Me, though he may die, he shall live." John 11:25

For as the Father raises the dead and gives life to them, even so the Son gives life to whom He will. John 5:21

Foundational Step #3: Dance of Lyrics

Hundreds of studies have shown that lyrics or words powerfully influence thinking, behavior, and mood, and much of it occurs without conscious awareness. We listen to favorite songs and hum along with them. A commercial with a catchy jingle has us singing along and possibly influences our buying choices.

We all have life lyrics that play over and over in our head or heart. "I have to perform," "No one loves me," "There is something wrong with me," "I am always on the outside," "I never fit in," "I have to win," or "I cannot fail."

Life lyrics cause us to respond in certain ways

Researchers have discovered that music and lyrics create "priming." This is when a person is exposed to certain stimuli such as words, lyrics, or surroundings, and their subconscious mind is activated. Once activated, the person's behavior, actions, or attitudes come out in ways that are consistent with the stimulus without awareness of why they are behaving in that manner.

Circle all the lyrics you have:

- I am not enough
- I am flawed
- I am not good enough
- I have to perform
- I am afraid of rejection
- I am afraid of failure
- I am afraid of abandonment
- I must protect my "family secrets"
- My thoughts, feelings and perceptions are wrong or unacceptable

- I need to hide my shame from others
- It was my fault
- I worry what others think
- I am a victim

Write down other ones:

_____

_____

_____

Prayer:

Father,

You see my lyrics or beliefs of shame. Even though the enemy has tried to replant lyrics of shame, I chose to uproot and replace them with Your Word. Your Word is light, and darkness and my shame was nailed to the cross of Jesus. Because of His death I am not flawed but accepted in The Beloved. He has declared me to white as snow. Your truth will set me free.

The Beloved's Lyrics (adapted from scripture):

Circle the ones that apply to you: IMPORTANT TO READ THESE LYRICS OUT LOUD UNTIL YOU BELIEVE IN YOUR HEART. (Initially, you may not believe what you are speaking, but FAITH

COMES BY HEARING). God's Word will not come back to Him void but will fulfill its intention.

- I am righteous and free of blame because through Jesus's death He has declared me to be holy and blameless. Col 1:22
- I am righteous because God, in His grace, freely makes me right in his sight. He did this through Christ Jesus when He freed us from the penalty for our sins. Rom 3:24 ((New Living Translation))
- I am righteous because God has called me a tree of righteousness. Is. 61:3
- I am righteous because God is my righteousness. Jer. 23: 6 (New Living Translation)
- I am righteous because God counted my faith as righteousness. Rom. 4:22
- I am righteous because of God's wonderful grace and His gift of righteousness. Rom.5:17 (New Living Translation)
- I am righteous because God lives in me, and I have been made right with God. Rom 8:10 (New Living Translation)
- I am righteous because I am accepted in *The Beloved*. Eph. 1:6
- I am righteous because I live in truth because God's Word is setting me free. John 8:32
- I am not flawed because God says I am a masterpiece. Eph 2:10

Prayer:

Holy Spirit,

Thank You that You are the power that raised Christ from the dead, and You are working in me. As I read and speak Your Word over me, let the power of Your righteousness be released in my heart and life. Let these new lyrics produce the life-changing fruit of Your righteousness in my life.

Foundational Step #4: Dance of Forgiveness

Forgiveness of our self and others is essential to learning how to dance with *The Beloved*. Unforgiveness impacts our spiritual, physical, and emotional health. It keeps us in prison and subject to being tormented by *The Deceiver*.

Who made you feel shame? Parent, caregiver, teacher, employer, family member?

List their names here:

_____

_____

_____

If it is difficult to think about forgiving someone, go back and reread *Chapter Four: Foundational Step 4: Dance of Forgiveness.* You forgive until all the pain is gone. For me, there was so much bitterness. I was forgiving a hundred times a day. The pain left, and *The Deceiver's* attempts to torment me left.

Prayer:

Father,

I choose to forgive these people because I know it will set me free from the pain of shame. This doesn't justify their sin, but rather takes away the power of shame has had over me.

I choose forgiveness because it is what You want me to do. I don't want to be tormented by The Enemy (The Deceiver) any longer. I want out of the prison of shame within my soul. I don't want to be his puppet and controlled any longer. Holy Spirit, thank You that You will remind me every time I feel shame, dirty, or flawed in my heart. Help me when I don't want to forgive. Wash my heart clean and remove the stain of bitterness from my heart

* * *

Dance with *The Beloved*

Precious looks down and finally sees Jesus's Robe of Righteousness. She knows that she is still flawed but knows His grace and love covers her completely. As they dance, The Beloved sings songs over her. Beautiful melodies of redemption flood her heart. His Words wash over like a gentle, cleansing rain. They remind her of her worth and value. "You are beautiful and precious in My sight, and all I see are

My Son's righteousness." Perfect love delivers her from fear or rejection and abandonment. Precious is safe and sheltered in the arms of The Beloved.

* * *

Dance your way to freedom! Envision yourself as the dancer.
https://mariplanklifecoach.com/
dance-of-righteousness-overcoming-shame/

CHAPTER SIX

DANCE OF SECURITY: OVERCOMING INSECURITY

You'd find me in a minute—you're already there waiting!

Then I said to myself, "Oh, He even sees me in the dark!

At night I am immersed in the light!"

Ps. 139:10–11 The Message. Bible

Love letter from heaven:

Precious One,

How I long for you to be free of insecurity. I long for you to know the powerful work of My perfect love which drives out all fear. I am your Good Shepherd and concerned with your care and wellbeing. I understand how bothersome, destructive, and oppressing insecurity can be. I have come to set you free and teach you the Dance of Security. You are secure in Me. I am your refuge and fortress. You matter. You have a voice. You are not invisible.

* * *

Precious and The Deceiver begin the dance. Insecurity has made her feel invisible. She doesn't count. Her voice is left unheard. The Deceiver comes to steal, kill, and destroy Precious. He knows the power of insecurity and how to wield it as an effective weapon and trap. His goal is to encase her in darkness.

The Deceiver is quick to point out everyone around her who has met the "the standard." They have success, appearance, or recognition. Bitterness and resentment flood her soul. "It is not fair that they made it." Following the endless comparisons is self-hatred, condemnation, and depression. The pit of insecurity grows deeper and darker.

Pretend and cover up. That is all Precious has done in the past. Her feeble attempts make The Deceiver laugh, and he tells her, "It is still there. No matter how much you try and hide or cover up, everyone knows how flawed you really are."

* * * *

What is insecurity?

Insecurity is a feeling of uncertainty, a lack of confidence or anxiety about yourself. Someone who doesn't have self-confidence is full of doubts about themselves. They feel like everyone judges or condemns them. Insecurity is a universal human frailty.

Where did it begin?

We can trace the beginning of insecurity to Adam and Eve. The Fall of Man was the turning point for all of us. This was where insecurity became a part of the human DNA. As a result, insecurity has passed down through the generations and taken on different forms within individuals and families. Let's take a look at what happened prior to the Fall.

In Genesis 1 we see God creating light, division of night and day, land, and sea. Then we see trees, plants, animal and sea life, and the sun and moon coming into existence. God pronounced, "It was good," six times during the creation process. (The word "good" or tohv in Hebrew means good, goodness, whatever is pleasant or happy.)

Genesis 1:26–29 was the creation of mankind. Up to this point creation resulted from God speaking: *"Let there be…."* Now in vs. 26 God says, *"Let Us make man in Our image, according to Our likeness; let them have dominion over the fish of the sea, over the birds of the air, and over the cattle, over all the earth and over every creeping thing that creeps on the earth."* In vs. 27 God says, *"So God created man in His own image; in the image of God He created him; male and female He created them."*

In Genesis 2:7 it says, *"And the Lord God formed man of the dust of the ground and breathed into his nostrils the breath of life; and man became a living being."*

Why is this so important?

Mankind was the final and crowning glory of God's creation. We are distinct from the rest of creation. The Divine Triune Godhead ("Let Us") determined that man was to have God's image and likeness.

We were not made to be a "god" but to reflect our Creator. We are spiritual beings with a soul and body. He gave us intelligence, personality, perception, and self-determination. He gave us emotions such as compassion, love, joy—just like Himself.

At this point, we were perfect and not marred with the consequences of sin. All of the expressions we learned of insecurity were not present. All man knew was perfect love reflecting in his relationship with God and with each other.

We see in Genesis 2:25 that Adam and Eve were both naked and were not ashamed. There was no need to hide or cover up. There was no fear, guilt, or compensating for insecurity. They were without sin, and there was a beautiful intimacy between them and God. They would walk in the cool of the day with God. He would come down and fellowship with them on a regular basis. Genesis 3:8 says that after the Fall, "And they heard the sound of the Lord God walking in the garden in the cool of the day, and Adam and his wife hid themselves from the presence of the Lord God among the trees of the garden."

God breathed into our nostrils His breath of life or the Holy Spirit. Unlike the rest of creation, a human being was created in covenant relationship to God and has an exceptional high and distinct value, purpose, and authority. We were given

- His image and likeness. Gen. 1:26
- His breath or Holy Spirit. Gen. 2:7
- Authority over all the earth. Gen. 1:26
- Authority over all the animals as shown in Gen.2:20 where God brings them to Adam to name them. This also shows a beautiful relationship between God Creator and man. They were working in partnership.

Devastation of the Fall

Genesis 2:16, 17 tells us God gives them free will to eat of every tree in the garden, except the tree of the knowledge (da'at, means knowing, understanding, wisdom, intelligence, and discernment) of good (tohv means good, goodness, whatever is pleasant or happy) and evil (ra, evil something bad, tragedy, trouble, distress, something of poor quality). Partaking of this fruit would result in death.

In Genesis 3:5, the serpent (*The Deceiver*) tempts Eve to eat from the tree by telling her, *"For God knows that in the day you eat of it your eyes will be opened, and you will be like God, knowing good and evil." Eve saw the tree was good for food, pleasant to the eyes, and desirable to make one wise. She ate and gave some to*

Adam. (vs.6). He is lying to them. God never told them that they will become like Him. Rather, He said if they ate the fruit it would result in death (physical, spiritual, relational, emotional).

Their immediate response was the beginning of insecurity. Fear was the first response and insecurity resulted. It is my professional opinion that fear is at the root of the majority of our emotional, spiritual, and relational problems. Insecurity resulted, and as we learned earlier, many expressions of insecurity resulted causing much distress and trouble. Let's take a look at the immediate result of Adam and Eve disobeying God: Gen. 3:7–12

Awareness of vulnerability, trying to cover up, and shame. Then the eyes of both of them were opened, and they knew that they were naked; and they sewed fig leaves together and made themselves coverings. vs. 7

Hiding from God, fear of rejection. And they heard the sound of the Lord God walking in the garden in the cool of the day, and Adam and his wife hid themselves from the presence of the Lord God among the trees of the garden. Then the Lord God called to Adam and said to him, "Where are you?" vs. 8, 9

Fear and hiding. So, he said, "I heard your voice in the garden, and I was afraid because I was naked; and I hid myself." vs. 10

Blaming, pointing fingers. And He said, *"Who told you that you were naked? Have you eaten from the tree of which I commanded* *you that you should not eat?" Then the man said, "The woman whom you gave to be with me, she gave me of the tree, and I ate." vs. 11, 12*

My testimony:

I understand the prison of insecurity. I always felt the need to perform for approval. I was raised to believe the importance of education and achievement. Performance for acceptance in every area of my life was a driving force. The more insecure I felt, the more I performed.

Another expression of my insecurity was the need for love. Insecurity, low self-esteem, codependency, the need for love plus the generational curse of domestic violence gave The Deceiver a huge foothold and opportunity for destruction in my life. I found myself in a nine-year violent relationship that began in dating and continued through my marriage. The things I just mentioned played off each other and reinforced my victim mentality, depression, self-loathing, and powerlessness.

Dance of Security

What is security?

It is freedom from danger. It is safety and freedom from fear or anxiety. It is the measure of the stability of an individual's emotional state. It is freedom from feelings of vulnerability or inferiority. It is assurance you matter and have significance. God doesn't want you to feel invisible and have the need to hide behind "fig leaves."

Remember earlier we learned the root of insecurity is fear? It was the first reaction after mankind sinned. Insecurity has plagued us in various ways, for different reasons, but with a similar outcome.

Just like Adam and Eve, we hide, pretend, and cover up insecurity. They used figs leaves to protect themselves, but we resort to "creative" ways as our "fig leaves." Even with our most decorated and elaborate "fig leaves" we are left feeling vulnerable and exposed. This makes us want to cover up more.

How do we overcome insecurity?

Work on yourself. Diligently incorporate *The Dance of Freedom*, especially in the area of your lyrics and belief system. Recognize insecurity is a result of fear. God has not given you a spirit of fear, but of power, of love, and of a sound mind, according to 2 Tim. 1:7.

Stop looking to others to validate you. Remind yourself that God sees you as acceptable. ". . . to the praise of the glory of His grace, by which He made us accepted in *The Beloved*" Eph. 1:6. Give yourself some grace and keep reminding yourself that Jesus sees you as acceptable.

Is your mirror your enemy? Mirrors can be cruel. They show us every wrinkle, flaw, flab, etc. Stop with the self-hatred or self-loathing. God doesn't see your crow's feet, muffin top, thinning or gray hair. In fact, He sees you as His masterpiece, a beautiful tapestry or symphony!

"For we are God's masterpiece. He has created us anew in Christ Jesus, so we can do the good things He planned for us long ago." Eph. 2:10 NLT

God made you with His own hands and gave you His Spirit. You were made in the image of the Triune God. A masterpiece is a work done with extraordinary skill, a supreme intellectual or artistic achievement. That is, you! Just receive it! Not receiving God's truth is calling Him a liar. Ask the Holy Spirit to help you receive and believe!

There is nothing wrong with wanting to look our best. I wear makeup, try to exercise, and enjoy wearing clothes that flatter. I have learned to love myself as Christ loves me. It is not vanity, but God helping me not to hate myself.

When I look in the mirror and I see a new wrinkle, which seems to happen more often, I try not to go into self-loathing. When I do, I remind myself of Ps. 139: 14, "I will praise you, for I am fearfully and wonderfully made; Marvelous are your works."

Stop comparing yourself with others. Comparisons, or wishful thinking, "I wish I was…," "I would be better if…," "If only I was… then I could be …" are traps of *The Deceiver* with the intention to steal, kill, and destroy. All this will result in feeling worse and reinforce insecurity.

Remember, fear is the root of insecurity. My go-to scripture when any kind of fear tries to attack me is, "For God has not given us a spirit of fear, but of power and of love and of a sound mind" 2

Tim. 1:7. So much of my healing journey was dealing with all kinds of fear. These are the fears I was facing:

- Fear of failure
- Fear of rejection
- Fear of divorce
- Fear of staying married to Fred
- Fear of not making it
- Fear of Fred discovering where I was hiding when I ran away
- Fear of my kids becoming abusive
- Fear of the abuse
- Fear of the unknown

Repent of jealousy and bitterness toward others. These behaviors imprison your soul and reinforce insecurity.

In conclusion, insecurity is a feeling of uncertainty, a lack of confidence, or anxiety. Someone who doesn't have self-confidence is full of doubts about themselves. People who are insecure have a continual anxiety and fear that they are going to be found out and left behind. Fear is the root of insecurity. They often feel they are "not enough," "don't matter," or "do not have voice."

The root of insecurity is fear. It was the first reaction after mankind sinned. Insecurity has plagued us in various ways, for different reasons, but with similar outcome. Just like Adam and Eve, we hide, pretend, and cover up insecurity. They used figs leaves to protect themselves, but we resort to "creative" ways as our "fig leaves." Even with our most decorated and elaborate "fig leaves" we are left feeling vulnerable and exposed. This makes us want to cover up more.

The Beloved has not given you a spirit of fear, but of power, of love, and of sound mind. He is your refuge and high tower. You can rest confidently in the truth that you matter. You have a voice. There is no longer a need to "cover up" with your fig leaves. You are His workmanship created in Christ Jesus for good works.

* * *

Dance of Freedom

Let's take the four foundational steps and apply them to the *Dance of Acceptance*. Each step is important to the entire *Dance of Freedom*. Take some time to pray and ask the Holy Spirit to help you by revealing truth. God's truth will set you free.

And you shall know the truth, and the truth
shall make you free. John 8:32

Foundational Step #1: Dance of Awareness

The Dance of Awareness is important by understanding the relationship between our fruit (attitude, actions, emotions), our trunk (beliefs or lyrics), and our soil (relationships, events, circumstances).

Fruit: circle the fruit on your tree:

- Boast
- Bully others
- Compare
- Compensate
- Continual self-doubt
- Control
- Cover up
- Crave and seek approval
- Fear of failure
- Fear of rejection
- Feel insignificant
- Feel unworthy
- Focus on other's weaknesses to make ourselves look better
- Focus on others to meet your needs
- Hide
- Obsessed with image or appearance
- Passive
- Perform
- Plagued with fears
- Poor boundaries
- Pretend
- Surround ourselves with like-minded people
- Surround ourselves with people who we wish to be
- Worry about what others think
- Worship or idolize others

Prayer:

Father, you see my fruit of insecurity. Help me when I am afraid and vulnerable and cover up with my "fig leaves." Your perfect love casts out all fear. Holy Spirit, You are the power that raised Christ from the dead, and You dwell in me. Help me to use Your Word when I feel insecure and remind me of Your perfect love that casts out fear.

How insecurity affects our roots or soil

As insecurity is passed down and through our family tree, it makes its way into our soil or roots. Insecurity weaves itself in and through our childhood from past traumas and experiences. Failure or rejection, loneliness, social anxiety, and negative beliefs about yourself or perfectionism can occur.

What sources of insecurity are in your roots or soil? Circle all that apply:

- Abandonment (emotional or physical)
- Codependency
- Comparisons
- Critical parent or partner
- Cultural expectations
- Failures
- Judgment
- Mistakes

- People's opinions mattered
- Rejection
- Trauma
- Victimization

Prayer:

Father, You see my roots of insecurity. Thank You. I am a new crea-ture in You. Despite what caused insecurity You can heal me. I give You these roots and ask for Your healing through the precious blood of Jesus. I desire to be a tree planted by Your Living Water that is nourished and strengthened. Let Your redemptive work secured by Jesus's death and resurrection manifest in my roots. I want to be rooted securely and confidently in Your love.

Foundational Step #2: Dance of Words

Words have great power. They have the power to shape, influence, build, destroy, plant, and bring things into life. Think of the words you have heard. It doesn't matter if they came from people, *The Deceiver*, or yourself. You were influenced and affected by their power to create and maintain insecurity.

- Be invisible
- Compare
- Compensate
- Cover up
- Failure

- Flawed
- Hide
- Insignificance
- Lack
- Pretend
- Rejection
- Strive

Write down other words

_____

_____

_____

Foundational Step #3: Dance of Lyrics

Check all the lyrics you have:

- I am a victim
- I am afraid of abandonment
- I am afraid of failure
- I am afraid of rejection
- I am codependent
- I am flawed
- I am not enough
- I am not good enough
- I must perform

- I need others to validate me
- I worry what others think

There is someone who is_____ (better, stronger, more capable, accepted, favored, more attractive, smarter, FILL in the BLANK) than me.

Write down other ones:

_____

_____

_____

Prayer:

Father, You see my lyrics or beliefs of insecurity. Even though the enemy has tried to plant lyrics of insecurity, I choose to uproot and replace them with Your Word. Your Word is light, and darkness or insecurity cannot hide when I choose the light of Your Word. Thank You. Your truth will set me free.

The Beloved's Lyrics (adapted from scripture):

Circle the ones that apply to you: IMPORTANT TO READ THESE LYRICS OUT LOUD UNTIL YOU BELIEVE IN YOUR HEART. (Initially, you may not believe what you are speaking, but **FAITH COMES BY HEARING**). **God's Word will not come back to Him void but will fulfill its intention.**

- I am secure because I don't have the spirit of fear but power, love, and a sound mind. 1 Tim 1:7
- I am secure because I am an overcomer. Rom. 8:37
- I am secure and not helpless, because the Holy Spirit is my helper. John 14:16
- I am secure in the knowledge that I am accepted in *The Beloved*. Eph. 1:6
- I am secure because I live in truth because God's Word is setting me free. John 8:32
- I am secure because God says I am a masterpiece. Eph 2:10
- I am secure because God is my refuge. Ps. 91

Prayer:

Holy Spirit,

Thank You that You are the power that raised Christ from the dead, and You are working in me. As I read and speak Your Word over me, let the power of healing, transformation, renewal, regeneration be released in my heart and life. Let these new lyrics produce the fruit of Your righteousness in my life.

Foundational Step #4: Dance of Forgiveness

Forgiveness is essential to learning how to dance with *The Beloved*. Unforgiveness impacts our spiritual, physical, and emotional health. It keeps us in prison and subject to being tormented by *The Deceiver*.

Who made you feel insecure? Parent, caregiver, teacher, employer, family member?

List their name/names here:

_____

_____

_____

If it is difficult to think about forgiving someone, go back and reread *Foundational Step 4: Dance of Forgiveness*. You forgive until all the pain is gone. For me, there was so much bitterness; I was forgiving hundred times a day. The pain left, and *The Deceiver's* attempts to torment me left.

Prayer:

Father,

I choose to forgive _____ *because I know it will set me free from insecurity. I choose forgiveness because it* is what You want me to do. I don't want to be tormented by The Deceiver any longer. I want out of the prison within my soul. I don't want to be his puppet and controlled by insecurity.

Holy Spirit, show me any resentment, bitterness, or unforgiveness I may have. Wash my heart clean and remove the stain of bitterness from my heart. When I compare myself to others, remind me that I am a workmanship or masterpiece in Christ Jesus. I am fearfully and wonderfully made.

* * *

Dance with *The Beloved*

Precious and The Beloved begin to dance. At first, she still felt insecure, and fear gripped her heart. Precious becomes less invisible as she realizes her importance and value is based upon how The Beloved sees her. She has a voice and can be heard. As they continue to dance, she hears His lyrics of love, grace, and strength as beautiful melodies flood her soul and heart. There is perfect love from the Perfect Beloved.

Every place His light comes, insecurity and fear are driven out. Freedom and redemption bring her deliverance. "Let my daughter go" resound in her heart. Every step with The Beloved is now a Dance of Freedom.

* * *

Dance your way to freedom! Envision yourself as the dancer.

https://mariplanklifecoach.com/

dance-of-security-overcoming-insecurity/

CHAPTER SEVEN

DANCE OF POWER: OVERCOMING POWERLESSNESS

For God has not given us a spirit of fear, but of power and of love and of a sound mind. 2Tim. 1:7

Love letter from heaven:

Precious One,

I desire to fill you with my power through the Holy Spirit. He is the resurrection power and the one who raised Christ from the dead. You are more than a conqueror through my Son's victory at Calvary. I have come to restore your ability to walk as my Princess Warrior. You are strong in Me. You are able through Me. Be filled with My Holy Spirit and Word.

* * *

Precious and The Deceiver begin the dance. From head to toe chains wrap around her, immobilizing every step. She feels powerless, and the only choice is to follow his whim and will. Each link in the weighted chains has" fear" inscribed on it. It permeates her very soul and heart. The darkness produced by powerlessness is heightened by anxiety and worry. Every small ember of hope, healing, or deliverance is overcome by staggering darkness. She is helpless, hopeless, and powerless.

* * *

What is powerlessness?

It means to be without ability, influence, or power. It is feeling helpless, ineffective, useless, vulnerable, or defenseless. It feels like "I am a victim," "I have no choices," "I have no voice," "I am not recognized," "I am not seen, heard, or understood," "Someone or something has more power and influence over me." It feels like "I am stuck, defenseless, and helpless."

What makes us powerless?

Relationships, situations, illness, or death of a loved one can make us feel powerless. We've lost control. We had no say in what happened. We were the victims of circumstances or other people's actions.

What takes away our power?

Insecurity and low self-esteem. One of the common elements I have seen in myself and others is a pervasive sense of insecurity. Often, we attract others who will take advantage of our vulnerability. They manipulate, control, and use emotional blackmail or other means to keep us powerless. *The Deceiver* tells us our voice and need for respect and safety is invalid. Therefore, we have no right to ask for these things, especially in relationships.

Fear of the unknown. Not knowing what you don't know often increases anxiety and heightens fears. Without knowledge, we are subject to assumptions, fantasy thinking, or making emotional decisions. We think about the "worst-case scenario." This only keeps us in the heightened state of fear.

Codependency. In all relationships where there is an imbalance of power, codependency plays a major role. Our damaged sense of worth drives us to rescue, excuse, save, and overlook the other person's need for power and control.

Giving another person power over you. When I allow others to disrespect my person, boundaries, safety, or opinions, I am giving them power and control. I start to disappear and become invisible. What is left is their version of who I should be. This version always benefits them and diminishes me. A healthy relationship is always mutually beneficial to all parties.

Blaming others and not taking responsibility for our actions. I was an expert at blaming my abusive husband for all of our problems. I was a victim, and he was the abuser. It made sense that it was his entire fault. My dad told me he was sick of hearing excuses for my behavior. Wow! What a shocker! It was at that point I realized that it was time for no more excuses (blaming everyone else for my problems). The buck stops here. My healing continued when I took a good look at what I was doing and took responsibility for my actions.

Not making choices. Making a small one like reading a book on healing is a step in the right direction. The path to healing, deliverance, and freedom begins with a step. One of the scriptures that helped me was Deut. 30:19:

I call Heaven and Earth as Witnesses today against you,
that I have set before you life and death, blessing and cursing
therefore choose life; both you and your descendants may live.
Deut. 30:19

Fear. As Precious danced with *The Deceiver*, she remained powerless by chains of fear. Fear can be debilitating and immobilizing and a dark prison. My scripture for fear was:

For God has not given us a spirit of fear, but of power and of
love and of a sound mind. 2 Tim. 1:7

Example:

Michele and Alex are born-again believers, have served as leaders in their church, and have two wonderful children. Michele is beautiful, confident, and full of life. Her fifteen-year marriage has been marked with emotional abuse and reduced her to feeling powerless, worn down, depressed, stuck, and bulldozed.

Alex's continual unwillingness to compromise, interpret Michele's feelings, and project and blame is emotional abuse. They play out the abuse cycle over and over. Things seem okay for a season, but true to the nature of an abusive relationship, the destructive cycle continues.

Michele and I have had conversations throughout her marriage. She was given suggestions to improve communication, but more importantly, she needed to regain her power. For fifteen years she had felt helpless, afraid, and stuck. Once again, she reached a point where divorce seemed like the only way out. Michele knew she had to do things differently if she wanted different results. She identified areas which contributed to her powerlessness and what she would do differently.

Financial dependence upon *Alex. She had a desire to go to back to school and get a degree, which would make her more financially independent. Historically, whenever she tried to pursue an education, Alex would tell her she needed to wait. Now she is pursuing her education and has found a way to pay for it without Alex's help.*

No plans for change. *Now Michele set a course of action toward her goals and is implementing them, one step at a time.*

Allowing fear of the unknown to immobilize her. *Now Michele combats the fear of the unknown by getting the necessary information needed for her action steps. The feelings of fear are still there, but she moves through the fear rather than allow it to keep her in the same place.*

Playing her part in the abusive cycle. *(More information about abuse cycles in this chapter.) In the past they would repeat the abusive cycle. She would get fed up and threaten divorce. Alex would change for a moment, causing Michele to back down. Now she recognizes when they are in the "honeymoon phase" of the abuse cycle and is committed not to make emotional decisions about Alex's "change." We discussed that true change takes time and needs to be sustained over a period of time. She cannot believe his promises of change anymore. She has to see it in sustainable action.*

Fear. *Before, fear would keep her from moving forward. Now she recognizes her fear and has the courage to keep walking forward even though she is feeling fearful.*

Not making choices. *Alex's continual bulldozing of Michele's opinions and feelings stopped her ability to make choices. Now she continues to make more choices about moving forward.*

Giving into Alex's promises of change. *Before, she would believe Alex's promises of change and relinquish her need for mutually* shared power in the relationship. Now, she has set a clear way to see if Alex's professed changes will be sustained over a period of time. Regardless of whether he changes or not, she is taking her power back and moving forward.

Weak or ambiguous boundaries. Michele has set clear boundaries with Alex of what she is willing and not willing to do. His choices will determine her choices.

Michele states she feels more empowered, stronger, and free. The vibrant, confident woman is coming back from powerlessness. She still encounters fear and some of the old feelings but is not allowing them to be her motivation.

My testimony:

I understand powerlessness. As a victim of domestic violence, I was powerless for quite a while. I was defenseless against the physical and emotional abuse from my husband, and my solution was to leave with my kids throughout our five-year marriage.

Usually, the abuse would occur when he was doing drugs. But sometimes out of the blue an assault would occur. I was always on edge, trying to keep peace and stay out of his way. Abusers take away support systems and finances and continually wear one down with criticism, shame, and guilt, which only reinforces "victim mentality." My self-esteem was already pretty low, and those things continued to diminish it away.

I felt powerless for a long time. I had given my power to my ex-husband. I had given it to my circumstances. I had given my power to the enemy whose only plan was to steal, kill, and destroy, according to John 10:10

Signs of emotional abuse

The abuser will tell blatant lies. You know it is an outright lie. Yet they are telling you this lie with a straight face. Why are they so blatant? They're setting up a precedent. Once they tell you a huge lie, you're not sure if anything they say is true. Keeping you unsteady and off-kilter is the goal.

The abuser denies they ever said something, even though you have proof. You know they said they would do something, and you know you heard it. But they deny it. It makes you start questioning your reality—maybe they never said that thing. And the more they do this, the more you question your reality and start accepting theirs.

The abuser will use what is near and dear to you as ammunition. They know how important your kids are to you, and they know how important your identity is to you. So those may be one of the first things they attack. If you have kids, they tell you that you should not have had those children. They will tell you'd be a worthy person if only you did not have a long list of negative traits. They attack the foundation of your being.

The abuser will wear you down over time. This is one of the insidious things about emotional abuse—it is done gradually, over time. A lie here, a lie there, a snide comment every so often, and then it starts ramping up. Even the brightest, most self-aware people can be sucked into emotional abuse. It is that effective. It is the "frog in the frying pan" analogy: The heat is turned up slowly, so the frog never realizes what's happening to it.

The abuser's actions do not match their words. When dealing with an emotionally abusive person or entity, look at what they are doing rather than what they are saying. What they are saying means nothing; it is just talk. What they are doing is the issue.

The abuser throws in positive reinforcement to confuse you. This person or entity that is cutting you down, telling you that you don't have value, is now praising you for something you did. This adds an additional sense of uneasiness. You think, "Well maybe they aren't so bad." Yes, they are. This is a calculated attempt to keep you off-balance—and again, to question your reality. Also look at what you were praised for; it is probably something that served the abuser.

The abuser knows confusion weakens people. Abusers know that people like having a sense of stability and normalcy. Their goal is to uproot this and make you constantly question everything. And humans' natural tendency is to look to the person that will help you feel more stable—and that happens to be the abuser.

The abuser will project. They are a drug user or a cheater, yet they are constantly accusing you of that. If you accuse them of something, they will quickly point the finger at you. This is done so often that you start trying to defend yourself and are distracted from the abuser's own behavior.

The abuser will try to align people against you. Abusers are masters at manipulating and finding the people they know will stand by them no matter what—and they use these people against you. They will make comments such as, "This person knows that you're not right," or "This person knows you're useless too." Keep in mind it does not mean that these people actually said these things. Abusers are constant liars. It makes you feel like you don't know who to trust or turn to—and that leads you right back to the abuser. That's exactly what they want because isolation gives them more control.

The abuser will tell you or others that you are crazy or have emotional problems. This is one of the most effective tools of the abuser, because it is dismissive. The abuser knows if they question your sanity, people will not believe you when you tell them the person is abusive or out of control. It is a master technique.

The abuser will tell you everyone else is a liar or they are wrong. By telling you that everyone else (your family, the media, counselors, etc.) is a liar, it again makes you question your reality. You've never known someone with the audacity to do this, so they must be telling the truth, right? No. It is a manipulation technique. It makes people turn to the abuser for the "correct" information—which isn't correct information at all.

Signs of physical abuse

Obvious signs of physical abuse are often physical in nature. These may include the following:

- Black eyes
- Bruises
- Burns
- Cuts
- Delay between the time of injury and the seeking of treatment; this may be because the victim is unable to leave the house for treatment or due to the shame felt over the abuse
- Name-calling and put-downs, overt anger, threats, attempts to intimidate by the abuser
- Overt jealousy or possessiveness over the victim
- Restraint or grip markings
- Restricting the victim's access to money
- Restricting the victim's movements (preventing them from attending work or school, controlling what they do or say)
- The abuser harming other people or animals in the victim's life

- The victim's noncompliance with a treatment regimen such as missed medical appointments or an inability to take medication due to lack of access to money
- Unusual pattern of injury; repeated trips to the emergency room
- Victim's fear of disagreeing with her abuser
- Victims will try to cover them up so as to hide the abuse due to fear of the abuser or shame about the abuse
- While physical violence is never okay, and physical abuse is never the fault of the victim, many victims feel the abuse is their fault

https://www.healthyplace.com/abuse/adult-physical-abuse/signs-of-physical-abuse-physically-abused-adults, accessed 2019.

Abuse cycle:

Honeymoon Phase- everything is wonderful, life is good, promises of change are made, abuser shows signs of remorse for abuse.

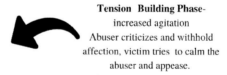

Tension Building Phase- increased agitation Abuser criticizes and withhold affection, victim tries to calm the abuser and appease.

Acting Out Phase- abuse occurs, tries to humiliate or blame victim, makes excuses for behavior.

My testimony:

I was caught in the abuse cycle. I would believe promises of change and was persuaded by "good behavior", and things would be wonderful for a season. Tension-building phase occurs then. He would act out and become abusive. I would leave until the next honeymoon phase occurred. The cycle repeated itself for nine years.

The Lord made it clear that the sin of domestic violence would pass from Fred to me to my children. I would not raise my boys to abuse their wives. My motivation was clear. The problem was I did not know how to get out of the abuse cycle. I told the Lord, I know the whys, but I need to know how to stay gone permanently.

God told me to be teachable and repentant. I had to stop blaming people for my problems. He told me to stop making emotional decisions. I realized my returning during the honeymoon phase was based upon feelings, not facts. I finally saw The Deceiver's game plan.

I learned that it takes eighteen months of counseling for most abusive men to become different. This is true for all types of abuse. I told Fred I would consider reconciliation if he was in therapy for at least eighteen months and I saw sustained change over a long period of time. True to his history, his professed changes fizzled out after a few months. This time I did not repeat our history by making emotional decisions based upon promises.

What is power?

A powerful person isn't someone with big muscles, military strength, or aggression. I am talking about my own power to make choices. I couldn't control my circumstances or my husband. I couldn't change him, despite my codependent frenzy! I only had power over my choices, actions, attitudes, words, and reactions.

The more I understood the power of God's love in my life and His acceptance, the more powerful I became. Why? The roots of insecurity and fear were getting healed. My confidence grew. I was assured of God's love. I became more confident in my right to have my own opinion and thoughts and to be the person God desired for me to become. I became confident in who God was making me to be and how He saw me.

As my confidence grew in the Lord so did my ability to make choices. It started out with small ones and grew bigger. Eventually over the course of time, through a series of choices, I was able to leave my abusive husband and marriage.

God was helping me set boundaries by learning to say "no" to victimization, codependency, helplessness, and powerlessness. 'No" was my new power word! I was saying "no" to everything! God lovingly told me I should learn "maybe." It was not saying "maybe" to powerlessness but becoming balanced in my newfound ability to set boundaries.

What is healthy balance of power in relationships?

- Clear communication: "I want," "I feel," "I need."
- Compromise
- Forgiveness
- Freedom to be yourself
- Fun
- Laughter
- No belittling, "put downs," name-calling
- No control or manipulation
- No hidden agendas or manipulation
- Respect boundaries, safety, opinions, feelings
- Shared decision-making
- They don't try and bulldoze you over with relentless questions, accusations, or judgments
- They don't try to interpret your feelings or opinions

You are worthy to have this in all your relationships. These represent God's best for you. Get healed because you will continue to attract others who will not be able to give these to you. Your emotional, spiritual, and relationship health will determine whom you attract.

Also, these are good things to work on yourself so that you can give these to others. A healthy balance of power in a relationship has to come from both parties.

What is courage?

"Courage is not the absence of fear but rather the judgment that something is more important than fear; the brave may not live forever but the cautious do not live at all."
Princess Diaries—The Movie

I love this quote! Courage is not the absence of fear but believing that something is more important than fear itself. I was filled with so much fear, but I could not allow *The Deceiver* to make me powerless. God gave me the courage, despite my fear.

Despite the numerous times I failed, God still helped me cross the finish line. I could not live with myself if my boys turned out abusive knowing that I could have stopped it from impacting future daughters-in-law and grandchildren. Sin passes down through generations. God told me Fred's sin of abuse would pass from him to me and to my children. The following scripture is the reason why sin, addictions, abuse, patterns of behavior, and repeated family dysfunction shows up generation after generation.

keeping mercy for thousands, forgiving iniquity and transgression and sin, by no means clearing the guilty, visiting the iniquity of the fathers upon the children and the children's children to the third and the fourth generation. Exo. 34:7

My emotional health was more important than fear. I was determined to understand how and why I became a victim. The Lord used books and His Word to give understanding and wisdom in the areas I needed. I used the *Dance of Awareness* during my healing journey I use it even today to address personal issues and help my coaching clients.

My relationship health was more important than fear. Understanding codependency was a huge eye-opener into the "whys" of my victimization. Blaming Fred kept me trapped. Truth was setting me free. The Holy Spirit was helping me in every area of twisted relationships. As my healing grew, so did my ability to have healthy relationships. The extent of my healing was reflected in my relationships. They become healthier and more satisfying.

My spiritual health was more important than fear. I have said this repeatedly but understanding and believing God's unconditional love is paramount and essential for healing. When I discovered the truth in Eph. 1:6, it became life-changing. It became a foundational principle for my counseling, book writing, clients, and personal healing. Heart knowledge of this truth will heal all insecurity, low self-esteem, fear of rejection, as well as codependency. I read and spoke this scripture until I believed it in my heart.

The future of my children was more important than fear. The warning God gave me and the scripture in Exo. 34:7 was clear. Allowing domestic violence in my life would allow this sin to pass to my children and grandchildren. I could never live with daughters-in-law or grandchildren suffering as I did.

keeping mercy for thousands, forgiving iniquity and transgression and sin, by no means clearing the guilty, visiting the iniquity of the fathers upon the children and the children's children to the third and the fourth generation. Exo. 34:7

What does the *Dance of Power* look like?

- The power to choose
- The power to believe *The Beloved* instead of *The Deceiver*
- The power to pursue wholeness
- The power to pursue a different path
- The power to choose God's truth over the lies
- The power to say "yes"
- The power to say "no"
- The power to choose joy or love
- The power to be strong because of Jesus
- The power to set boundaries and have them respected
- The power to become God's best version of myself
- The power to make mistakes and not be "perfect"
- The power to have and pursue your dreams
- The power to have healthy relationships
- The power to be financially independent
- The power to *Stop Dancing with the Enemy*
- The power to stop blaming others and take responsibility for my actions, attitudes, and beliefs

- The power to forgive and not be tormented through unforgiveness

In conclusion, powerlessness is to be without ability, influence, or power. It is feeling helpless, ineffective, useless, vulnerable, or defenseless. It feels like "I am a victim," "I have no choices," "I have no voice," "I am not recognized," "I am not seen, heard, or understood," "Someone or something has more power and influence over me," "I have no choices." It feels like "I am stuck, defenseless, and helpless."

God gives us the ability to have power through Him. The power to choose, overcome fear, and become rooted in His love. We can have relationships where there is healthy and mutual sharing of power. He has not given us the spirit of fear, but of power, of love, and of a sound mind. He sets before us the choice of life or death, blessings or cursing.

* * *

Dance of Freedom

Let's take the four foundational steps and apply them to the Dance of Power. Each step is important to the entire Dance of Freedom. Take some time to pray and ask the Holy Spirit to help you and reveal the truth. God's truth will set you free.

And you shall know the truth, and the truth shall make you free. John 8:32

Don't let *The Deceiver* derail you out of the *Dance of Freedom* through lies. He is a liar. Recognize some of his attempts to stop your *Dance of Freedom*.

- Feelings of condemnation, shame, or guilt
- It is all your fault
- It is hopeless
- What's the point?
- You will never change

Foundational Step #1: Dance of Awareness

The Dance of Awareness is important because it helps us to understand the relationship between our fruit (attitudes, actions, emotions), our trunk (beliefs or lyrics), and our soil (relationships, events, circumstances).

Fruit: Circle the fruit on your tree:

- Afraid
- Codependency
- Denial
- Helpless
- Hopeless
- Powerless
- Run over

- Stuck
- Victim

Prayer:

Father,

You see the fruit that is on my tree, and I desire Your fruit. Holy Spirit, release Your power, love, and grace in my life. Transform me from the inside out. Let Your truth set me free. Let Your love penetrate my heart and soul so I will know my worth and value. I can do all things through Christ who strengthen me. I choose Your power rather than powerlessness.

What are your roots from your past or relationships? Circle what applies:

The roots are the channels that extract nutrients from the soil and nourish the entire tree. Our soil can be culture, relationships, how we were raised, experiences, etc. Soil feeds our trunk or beliefs, then produces fruit. HOWEVER, we can be changed through the Word of God resulting in good fruit such as peace, love, joy, self-control, patience, goodness, healing, deliverance, healthy relationships, etc.

- Codependency
- Controlling relationships
- Emotional, sexual, or physical abuse
- Feelings, opinions, etc. are diminished or criticized

- Insecurity
- Insignificance
- Low self-esteem
- Not allowed to make choices
- Patterns of feeling powerless, helpless, victimized

Prayer:

Father, You see my roots of powerlessness. Uproot fear and insecurity. Saturate my roots with Your love and Word. Help me to see myself as able and confident through Your Holy Spirit. I can do all things through You. You destroyed powerlessness on the cross.

Foundational Step #2: Dance of the Word

Words have great power. They have the power to shape, influence, build, destroy, plant, and bring things into life. Think of the words you have heard. It doesn't matter if they came from people, *The Deceiver*, or yourself. You were influenced and affected by their power.

Circle the words of powerlessness you have heard:

- Crazy
- Fear
- Inadequate
- Insignificant
- No choice

- Stuck
- Victim
- Who would believe you?
- Without choices
- You are always wrong

Write down other ones:

_____

_____

_____

Prayer:

Father,

You see the words of powerlessness that have impacted me. You know the destruction it has caused. Forgive me for listening to them. Help me to cling to Your Word. Holy Spirit, give me a desire and passion to speak Your Word over and over until it produces the fruit of righteousness within. Thank You for Your power You give me through Your love, Word, and the Holy Spirit. I refuse to allow powerlessness to reign in my heart any longer.

Foundational Step #3: Dance of Lyrics

Hundreds of studies have shown that lyrics or words powerfully influence thinking, behavior, and mood, and much of it occurs without conscious awareness. We listen to favorite songs and hum along with them. A commercial with a catchy jingle has us singing along and possibly influences our buying choices. We all have life lyrics that play over and over in our head or heart.

Life lyrics cause us to respond in certain ways

Researchers have discovered that music and lyrics create "priming." This is when a person is exposed to certain stimuli such as words, lyrics, or surroundings, and their subconscious mind is activated. Once activated, the person's behavior, actions, or attitudes come out in ways that are consistent with the stimulus without awareness of why they are behaving in that manner.

How does powerlessness affect my lyrics or beliefs? Circle all the lyrics you believe:

- I am a victim
- I am always in unhealthy relationships
- I am bound by fear
- I am codependent
- I am helpless
- I am powerless
- I cannot set boundaries

- I feel hopeless
- I have no choices
- I have no control
- I have no voice

Write down other ones:

_____

_____

_____

Prayer:

Father,

You see my destructive lyrics I have believed. Please forgive me for believing them more than Your truth. Holy Spirit, release Your power, love, and grace in my life.

Jerusalem will be told: Don't be afraid. Dear Zion, don't despair. Your God is present among you, a strong Warrior there to save you. Happy to have you back, He'll calm you with his love and delight you with his songs.

Zeph. 3:17 The Msg. Bible

The Beloved's Lyrics (adapted from scripture):

Circle the ones that apply to you: IMPORTANT TO READ THESE LYRICS OUT LOUD UNTIL YOU BELIEVE IN YOUR HEART. (Initially, you may not believe what you are speaking, but FAITH COMES BY HEARING). God's Word will not come back to Him void but will fulfill its intention.

- I am powerful because I don't have the spirit of fear but of power, of love, and of a sound mind. 2 Tim 1:7
- I am powerful because I am an overcomer. Rom. 8:37
- I am powerful because I can cooperate with God as He fulfills His plans for my life which is hope and a future. Jer. 29:11
- I am powerful and not helpless, because the Holy Spirit is my helper. John 14:16
- I am powerful because in my weakness, God is made strong. 2 Cor. 12:19
- I am powerful because I am secure in the knowledge that I am accepted in *The Beloved*. Eph. 1:6.
- I am powerful because I live in truth because God's Word is setting me free. John 8:32

Other lyrics:

- Through Jesus, I am powerful because I am not a codependent and can have healthy relationships where there is shared power, mutual respect, and satisfaction.
- Through Jesus, I am powerful without the need to be controlling, aggressive, pushy, or demanding. I can be flexible, gracious, kind, and tenderhearted.
- Through Jesus, I am powerful because I am not a victim or doormat.

Prayer:

Holy Spirit,

Thank You that You are the power that raised Christ from the dead, and You are working in me. As I read and speak Your Word over me, let the power of healing, transformation, renewal, regeneration be released in my heart and life. Let these new lyrics produce the fruit of Your righteousness in my life.

Foundational Step #4: Dance of Forgiveness

Forgiveness of self and others is essential to learning how to dance with *The Beloved*. Unforgiveness impacts our spiritual, physical, and emotional health. It keeps us in prison and subject to being tormented by *The Deceiver*.

Who made you feel powerless? Parent, caregiver, teacher, employer, family member?

List their names here:

_____

_____

_____

Prayer:

Father,

You know how hard this is. It isn't fair or just that I have to forgive the people I listed for taking my power. But I choose to forgive because I know it will set me free. I choose forgiveness because it is what You want me to do.

I don't want to be tormented by The Deceiver any longer. I want out of the prison within my soul. I don't want to be his puppet and controlled by bitterness, anger, or resentment. Holy Spirit, thank You for cleansing resentment and unforgiveness in my heart. Help me when I don't want to forgive. Wash my heart clean and remove the stain of bitterness from my heart. I take back my power to choose, change, and be transformed by Your love and Word.

* * *

Dance with *The Beloved*

Precious and The Beloved begin to dance. At first, she still felt chains immobilizing every step. Fear still gripped her heart. As they continued to dance, she heard His lyrics of love, grace, and strength as beautiful melodies flooding her soul and heart.

Precious began to sing with The Beloved. "I have freedom to choose." "I can be free from powerlessness." "I don't have the spirit of fear, but of power, love and a sound mind." "I am free from the prison." Sometimes she would pick up the familiar chains of powerlessness, but quickly she was reminded of His perfect love which casts out all fear. Every step with The Beloved is now a Dance of Freedom.

* * *

Dance your way to freedom! Envision yourself as the dancer.

https://mariplanklifecoach.com/

dance-of-power-overcoming-powerlessness/

CHAPTER EIGHT

DANCE OF IDENTITY: OVERCOMING MISTAKEN IDENTITY

For Jacob My servant's sake, and Israel My elect, I have even called you by your name; I have named you, though you have not known Me. Is. 45:4

Love letter from heaven:

Precious One,

I desire for you to know who you are as defined by My love and Word. You were once a pauper, but now you are My princess and My treasure. As you learn your new identity, it will satisfy the longing in your heart to know how deeply loved you are. It will answer the question of value and worth.

* * *

Precious and The Deceiver begin the dance in a hall of mirrors. The whirlwind of blurred images spins around causing dizziness and confusion, every image melting into the next. Precious gets glimpses of how she is defined by others, her past, relationships, and mistakes. As she glances into each mirror there is a gnawing emptiness as she attempts to answer the question, "Who am I?" Behind each mirror's reflection is a dark void.

Sadly, she turns to The Deceiver as he says, "All you see in these images of you is nothing. You are nothing but empty frame reflecting the impressions, ideas, and value of what others say, think, or believe about you."

* * *

The big question: Who am I?

This deep and philosophical question has been asked throughout history. Poets, philosophers, and psychologists have contemplated this question for days, weeks, and even years. Behind this question lie deeper questions such as

- Am I really loved?
- What is my significance?
- Who am I?
- Where do I belong?

Because we are unique and complex our identity can be more unclear, cloudy, or uncertain. It is similar to a puzzle. There are many pieces that define who we are, and the parts are interconnected to each other. Often puzzle pieces share similar colors just like our story. Different aspects of our life "color" other parts. Our pieces are

- Associations
- Attitudes
- Culture
- Education
- Experiences
- Family
- Interests
- Perceptions
- Personality
- Quirks
- Relationships
- Strengths
- Weaknesses

While these pieces of our identity are important and influential, they are external. They can change through time or circumstances. Our identity becomes subject to change. The question of "Who am I?" is constantly in a fluid state. It seems there is no sure answer to this important question.

My testimony:

My puzzle pieces were negatively colored by my domestic violence journey. It seemed everything was touched by it. Victimization colored my self-esteem and my relationship with the Lord. I identified myself as a victim.

Similarly, my healing also influenced my identity. It now has an overlay of restoration, renewal, and hope. My past is no longer painful. I remember the events, but they no longer create torment and limitations. My victim lens has been replaced by God's identity, His love and Word.

What is missing from our identity puzzle?

Within the center of the identity puzzle is a huge hole. There is a God-shaped vacuum created by the Creator. It is His intention to connect our puzzle pieces of our identity through Him.

It is His plan that our value and worth would be defined and determined by God Himself. We need an eternal perspective to see ourselves through God's definition of our identity and value. His view of us is permanent because He cannot change. There are no shadows, and no variations in the Lord.

I understand what it means to live as a Christian without heart knowledge of my identity in Christ. I struggled with fear of rejection and did not experientially understand God's unconditional love.

I knew it intellectually. I could quote John 3:16, but I did not really believe it. As a result, I had low self-esteem, insecurity, and deep hunger for approval. Therefore, let's compare some other ways we understand and answer the question of Who am I? We will compare the world's way (external) to God's way (eternal); we will see the superficial ways vs. meaningful and profound ways. God will show us his answers to these questions:

- Am I really loved?
- What is my significance?
- Where do I belong?
- Who am I?
- How does the world identify us?

The world identifies us by our name, qualities, or beliefs that make us different or similar. It might be an identity of interests. It could also be individuality, personality, distinctiveness, or uniqueness. Identity is the individual characteristics by which a person or thing is recognized. It is the way others know who I am.

It can be my present circumstances such as student, unemployed, mother, single, divorced, or married. It can be our past failures or successes. Other ways of identification are occupation, education, if we have children or grandchildren, culture, heritage, etc.

This way of identification is superficial and shallow. It answers certain questions about who we are, but it doesn't bring fulfillment or meet the deepest longings in our heart. It won't bring us healing or restoration, nor will it reveal How God truly sees us.

Our identity in Christ

Our identity in Christ is everything He did for us when He died and rose again. It is applying and taking ownership of the new position and privileges in Christ. It is drawing my identity from the King of Kings, *Alpha and Omega*, or Yahweh. Won't you rather have your identity determined by the Creator of heaven and earth rather than your driver's license?

The key is to understand the profound change occurring the second we became born-again. Living from our new identity will result in healing, wholeness, and God-determined worth and value. Fears are erased, the past is healed, and we have a new purpose for life. We can walk in new authority.

Where did our identity in Christ begin?

The moment you accepted Jesus as your Savior and became born-again, amazing things happened!

Delivered from the power of darkness and transported into God's kingdom. Col 1:13 tells us that we were delivered from the power of darkness and transported into God's kingdom. This is a picture of captives taken by another king; the captives are enslaved and forced to leave their homeland. We were imprisoned by sin. It was our ruler. We were subject to its desires, cravings, and passions.

He has delivered us from the power of darkness and conveyed us into the kingdom of the Son of His love. Col.1:13

When we got saved the power of sin was destroyed. Jesus defeated the death grip of sin. It is no longer our master and enslaving us. Now when we sin it is a choice. We were captives, and now Jesus the Redeemer has set us free from the captivity of sin and brought us into His kingdom!

Filled with the Holy Spirit. The same One who raised Christ from the dead now lives inside. That is amazing when you think about it! The Spirit of God is now a deposit guaranteeing our inheritance. We are being transformed into the image of Christ. He is changing us from the inside out. It is no longer I who lives, but Christ who lives in me.

Declared holy and blameless. God sees you as set apart for holy purposes. He sees you as pure. Your blame and shame are no longer an issue for God. According to Eph 1:4 His precious blood has covered it all. We don't have to fall prey to condemnation any longer!

Just as He chose us in Him before the foundation of the world, that we should be holy and without blame before Him in love,

Eph. 1:4

Given eternal life. We can live from spiritual, emotional abundance according to John 10:10. Eternal life is not just a promise for the future, but we can live in God's abundance right now.

> *The thief does not come except to steal, and to kill, and to destroy. I have come that they may have life, and that they may have it more abundantly.* John 10:10.

> *For God loved the world so much that He gave his one and only Son, so that everyone who believes in him will not perish but have eternal life.* John 3:16

Redemption through the blood and forgiveness of sins. We were bought back! God paid our debt. The charges against us were dropped! Our record has been erased. We have a clean slate.

> *In Him we have redemption through His blood, the forgiveness of sins, according to the riches of His grace.*
> Eph.1:7

The list is endless! We will discuss this further and how they relate to our identity. Everything God says about you is true. Every promise is yes and amen!

Worldly IDs vs. heavenly ID

We all have government-approved legal documents such as passports, drivers' licenses, and social security cards. These are used to open accounts and get loans and jobs. We present these IDs when we use a credit card or write a check. They have facts such as name, birth date, address, and numbers assigned specifically to us. No one shares these documents. They are uniquely given to us.

Heavenly ID

Our new legal documents are our adoption papers! The moment we became born-again, we were legally adopted by God the Father. Definition of adoption is to take by choice into a relationship; especially, to take voluntarily (a child of other parents) as one's own child. An adopted child has all the legal rights as a natural child and is an heir to the Father's wealth and property. All that belongs to the Father belongs to us.

Having predestined us to adoption as sons by Jesus Christ to Himself, according to the good pleasure of His will. Eph. 1:5

You are no longer a "slave" but a son of the Most High God. And God does not just call you His son. He also calls you "an heir" through Christ. (Galatians 4:7) In fact, Romans 8:17 says that you are "joint heirs" with Christ.

Belonging and association create identity

We all want to belong, so we develop associations through friendships, relationships, connections, or involvement. It is an alliance.

You can tell a lot by someone's associations. We hang out with people like ourselves.

People can identify who I am by political party, special interests, friends, or hobbies. Also, by the places I attend on a frequent or consistent basis. The groups we invest time and energy in such as community organizations or church reveal who I am. We are drawn to groups based upon similarity. Those common shared beliefs create belonging.

You are a part of God's family. You are God's child and a part of His family. We belong to Him! He is our heavenly Father and committed to our care, growth, and provision. God sees us through Jesus. When Jesus was baptized, the Father announced that "This is My Beloved Son in whom I am well pleased." The way the Father loves Jesus is the way the Father loves you.

God has accepted you as a part of His family. He shows no partiality among His children. The exact measure of Christ's acceptance by God the Father is exactly how much you are accepted by Him.

We are partakers of God's new covenant. In the general sense, a covenant is simply a binding agreement or contract between two or more parties; in legal terms, it is a formal sealed agreement or contract. In fact, the Old and New "Testaments" are really the Old and New "Covenants"—the new covenant being of course that which was established by Christ through His shed blood for the remission of sins (Matthew 26:28).

The amazing thing about such examples of divine covenant is that they are the gracious means of relationship with God for a people who deserve to be removed from His presence forever, by a God who has no need whatsoever, in and of Himself, for such relationship. Indeed, the heart of covenant, as so often and wonderfully recapitulated by God Himself, is that expression of intimate relationship: "you will be my people, and I will be-your-God" e.g., Jeremiah 30:22 www.theopedia.com/covenant/ date of access 2/17

Our new identity is established securely through Jesus's sacrificial death. We are the blessed recipients of a new covenant, adopted by God the Father, and joint heirs with Christ. Our new identity addresses heart issues of belonging, significance, value, unconditional love, and acceptance. It will eradicate fears and will truly answer the question

What keeps us from our identity?

There are many things that keep us from knowing our identity. We will take some time to look at them in the next few sections.

Lack of knowledge. Many believers are not aware of their identity in Christ. I was a Christian for many years before I understood it. Once I learned of my new identity, my walk with the Lord radically changed. The key was learning about God's unconditional acceptance as a part of my new identity. I went from victim to victorious. My self-esteem was a minus twenty. Now I like myself because of how God sees me.

Misplaced faith. We put our faith in something. To believe is to be firm, stable, firmly persuaded, believe solidly, or consider trustworthy. We are the sum total of our belief system. My beliefs define my perceptions, attitudes, responses, behaviors, relationships, fears, insecurities and possibly affect me physiologically. We put our faith in how the world defines who we are.

Example:

If I were bitten by a big black dog, I would believe all dogs, no matter size, breed, or color are dangerous. Based upon this belief, I now avoid dogs. When I get close to a dog, my heart starts to beat faster, and my stomach starts to churn. My belief that all dogs are dangerous is reinforced by my fear and anxiety. This makes my belief seem true because it "feels" true.

I believed I had to perform for approval. I was persuaded I had no value or worth. I did not know I had more faith in the lies of the enemy (anything contrary to God's Word) until I read the Word. The more I read the Word with intent to know it as "truth," the more I discovered I had an entire belief system of lies. I began to put my faith where it belongs, in Jesus, in His Word and in the power of His death and resurrection.

Speaking lies rather than truth. What is a lie? A lie is anything contrary to God's Word. The source is Satan. According to John 8:44, he is called the father of lies.

You are of your father the devil, and the desires of your father

you want to do. He was a murderer from the beginning, and

does not stand in the truth, because there is no truth in him.

When he speaks a lie, he speaks from his own resources, for he

is a liar and the father of it. John 8:44

Rather than speak what God says about our identity, we speak everything else. We speak and believe what we have heard or have been told. We are quick to put ourselves down. We speak the negative rather than God's Word. We are God's treasure. God calls us His workmanship, created in Christ Jesus, but we are unmerciful and condemning when we look in the mirror.

We also rehearse and speak what we have heard from others. Verbal and nonverbal messages are equally destructive in creating belief systems of lies. Nicknames, put-downs, insults, and judgments create soul wounds. Soul wounds often impact our identity and perceptions of worth and value.

Example:

Mary had a huge desire to be a Hollywood producer. Her family told her she would never make it in Hollywood. She left Cleveland and moved to Hollywood. The words her family spoke over her created, fear, doubt, insecurity, and low self-esteem. She was rehearsing what they spoke over her. She believed what she had heard. Consequently, she was kept out of Hollywood for twenty years.

Similarly, words are seed. We receive seed words of others, and we sow seeds with our mouth. Salvation began when we confessed Jesus as Lord (see Rom. 10:9). That confession was a seed sown in faith and produced a harvest of righteousness, blessings, identity, and eternal life.

The power of confession also works in the negative. We confess the negative or lies of *The Deceiver*, and we will reap exactly what has been sown.

Example:

Mary was reaping the fruit of the words she was speaking for twenty years. She was speaking negative beliefs and reaped exactly what she had been sowing with her words. She had no contracts and no equipment. She had nothing to show for twenty years of trying to get into Hollywood.

She also believed that she had no worth or value. She suffered from insecurity and low self-esteem and had misconceptions about who she was and who was God.

During our coaching sessions, she applied The Dance of Awareness. Mary's insecurity and low self-esteem has been transformed into confident security in her identity.

Example:

Mary was speaking and sowing word seeds. She was the sum of her belief system. She had become everything she had spoken over herself. She was speaking lies such as

- *Everyone has more value than me*
- *God is mad at me, and I have to be perfect*
- *I am not accepted*
- *I am not important*
- *I don't like myself*
- *I will never make it in Hollywood*
- *When bad things happen to me it is my fault*

When Mary repented for speaking these things and changed her word seeds to the Word of God, God opened the door to Hollywood. Two weeks later she went from no contracts to having contracts and connections. Before she had no equipment, and after our session, she had access to millions of dollars in equipment. Eight years later she is producing her movie.

Not relying on the Holy Spirit. As the third member of the Triune Godhead, the Holy Spirit is the One who raised Christ from the dead and lives within us if we are born-again. For so many years I have tried to become more like Jesus and forget to ask the Holy Spirit for His power. He reveals Jesus to us and reveals Jesus in and through us.

that the God of our Lord Jesus Christ, the Father of glory,
may give to you the spirit of wisdom and revelation in the
knowledge of Him, the eyes of your understanding being
enlightened; that you may know what is the hope of His
calling, what are the riches of the glory of His inheritance in
the saints, and what is the exceeding greatness of His power
toward us who believe, according to the working of His mighty
power which He worked in Christ when He raised Him
from the dead and seated Him at His right hand in the
heavenly places, Eph. 1:17–20

The Deceiver. He does not want us to know our identity. He is thrilled when we look to the world's ways of giving us identity. We are encouraged to look to possessions, titles, occupation, education, wealth, fame, or fortune. As we have discovered, this path only leads to dissatisfaction and an empty heart.

He knows firsthand what Jesus's death and resurrection has accomplished.. That is why he works so hard to convince us to search for identity and value through external means.

He uses hopelessness, condemnation, accusations, fears, and plans of destruction. He will use these weapons until we refuse to give him authority and power. When we stand, speak, and believe God's Word, we will defeat the enemy. Remember, according to Colossians 2:15, Satan was the one who was defeated at the cross and publicly humiliated when Jesus went to the cross.

Having disarmed principalities and powers, He made a public spectacle of them, triumphing over them in it. Col. 2:15

Mary's story:

When Mary first came to see me, she did not know her identity in Christ. She had misconceptions about who God was. She thought God was mad at her. Mary needed to be perfect in order to get His favor. She was insecure and very fearful. During the session we reestablished her identity in Christ. She repented for believing lies. Mary took back her rightful inheritance.

What happened was amazing! She became confident, powerful, and faith-filled, and overcame incredible fears by knowing her identity. She began to speak God's Word and believe what He said. This transformation propelled her into fulfilling her call and destiny as a Hollywood producer. It did not happen overnight, but Mary was diligent to continue the process.

Thinking we are never enough. Many of us feel we are never enough or are inadequate. There is the feeling that we are not sufficient or we lack something. We are always a step behind everyone else. We are not paupers but royalty. We do not need have a pauper mentality and live as if there is not enough. In Christ, we have all of our needs met through Christ Jesus. His promises are yes and amen.

"When you are trained or raised to feel insignificant, you develop survival skills to try and avoid the pain of that reality. A

pauper uses survival skills because he believes that life is one big 'dog eat dog' world. This poverty mentality is the primary attribute of a pauper. Whether a pauper had experienced poverty in his or her finances or in love and affirmation, all paupers have the common belief that there is never going to be enough for them. They live in fear, struggling with the feeling that the well is about to dry up"[1]

New identity = new worth and value

The world assigns value and worth to my identity. Unfortunately, we judge others based upon who they associate or identify with. Depending upon my judgment the person is good or bad, or right or wrong. I join or distance myself with identifying groups because I share or disagree with the qualities, beliefs, or values.

Therefore, my identity is directly tied to how I find worth and value. This means we have merit, significance, attraction, importance, and meaning. We all have value. The difference is who and how it is defined or determined.

How we "weigh" worth and value

This old-fashioned balance scale is a good illustration of how "value" is determined. Its parts include a fulcrum, a beam that balances on it, two pans at the ends of the beam to hold the materials to be weighed, and counterbalancing weights. The scales would tip up or down based upon weighed material.

Society, culture, family, or personal expectations place a predetermined "weight" on one side of our value scale. It could be education, career, achievements, success, fame, fortune, skill, contributions, accomplishments, athleticism, or intellect.

Our value is constantly measured against predetermined weights. It is great when the scales tip in our favor and we've exceeded the predetermined weight. But how long will that last? Careers can change. Achievements, success, and fame are diminished when the bigger, better, faster thing appears. It is a roller coaster of highs and lows and ups and downs.

I understand the rollercoaster ride of having my value determined by an external measure. My family determined value from education, success, achievement, intellect, area where we lived, and the cars we drove. Coupled with my need for approval, this roller coaster was one of performance, fear of failure, and striving for approval.

Equally, we are so quick to measure value when we compare ourselves to other people. Do I have more value because I have a master's degree than the homeless man on the street? Is my value less because I don't drive a Mercedes-Benz? Am I worth more on payday when there is money in the bank? Am I more valuable because I live here in the United States than those who live in Third World countries?

Mary's story:

Before our life-coaching session, Mary was very insecure about her value. She thought producers, directors, actors, and actresses all had more value because they are important or famous. This translated into being "star struck" in their presence.

When she was in the presence of these people, she was afraid of rejection and felt that she needed to esteem, idolize, and put them on a pedestal. The comparison was heightened because of her insecurity. The more famous they were, the less value she had. This comparison of values was not just with the people in Hollywood; it was with any-one who she perceived to be bigger, greater, stronger, or better.

In our sessions, as we addressed the fears of rejection and fail-ure, I pointed out to her that she had just as much right to be in the same room as a producer or a director because of the value that God has assigned to her because of Jesus.

Now, when she walks into a room of Hollywood "bigwigs," she feels a sense of equality in value and worth. I told her if the President United States were in this room, we would honor him, but before the Lord, we all have the same value. His title and position merits respect but will never determine his value before the Lord.

Because of the incredible sacrifice and preciousness of Jesus's death and resurrection, God now looks at born-again believers through Jesus. He doesn't see or judge our external value. The eter-nal value we have is determined by who lives in us, not our resi-dence, car, education, or achievements.

Therefore, if our identity is grounded in Christ, then it will never change. It isn't based upon external judgments, stock mar-ket, or the opinions of man. My value and worth are determined by God who is eternal and never changes. My identity now has been established through Jesus's death and resurrection.

How does God see me?

God sees me as holy and blameless. God sees us as holy, which means sacred, blessed, and set apart. In Jesus we are declared righteous and without sin. God sees His perfect Son. He sees us as virtuous and in right standing with Him. Remember, we are now heirs with Christ.

Just as He chose us in Him before the foundation of the world, that we should be holy and without blame before Him in love.

Eph. 1:4

Now when we sin, the Holy Spirit convicts us of our sin, but there is never a judgment laid against us as a person. He only addresses the sinful behavior. Condemnation is from the enemy, and he tries to lay judgment, blame, and guilt against us as a person: "You never," "You always," etc. Have you heard these accusations before?

According to Ps. 103:12 our sins which separated us are as far as the east is from the west. If this is true then who is bringing condemnation? *The Deceiver.* He has come to steal, kill, and destroy, but Jesus has come to give us eternal life (see John 10:10).

As far as the east is from the west, So far has He removed our transgressions from us. Ps. 103:12

I had a Christian client who committed a sin when he was younger but still believed twenty years later that his sin was so great, God could never forgive him.

For twenty years the enemy had him under so much guilt and condemnation. It created such a burden and heartache. He asked for forgiveness but couldn't believe God would forgive him.

I told him that Jesus died for all sin. There were no exceptions. His sin was not bigger than the blood of Jesus. He had to accept God's forgiveness or continue to allow the condemnation to run his life.

There is therefore now no condemnation to those who are in Christ Jesus, who do not walk according to the flesh, but according to the Spirit. Rom. 8:1

Every time Satan tries to throw a past mistake or a confessed sin in my face, I speak Rom. 8:1, which tells me that there is no condemnation for those in Christ Jesus. I also remind him of Col. 2:15. It says that he was made a public spectacle at the cross. He was humiliated and shamefully defeated.

Having disarmed principalities and powers, He made a public spectacle of them, triumphing over them in it. Col. 2:15

He gets quiet and stops hurling condemnation my way. I tell him every time he tries to bring condemnation or guilt my way, I am going to remind him of his shameful public defeat. Condemnation and guilt used to be a loud voice in my life. Not anymore!

God sees me as accepted. So much of my testimony and healing came from Eph. 1:2–6. We are not subject to value and worth judgments or comparisons of the world. Anything that is contrary to the Word of God does not determine our value.

Most of us struggle with fears of rejection. Many have experienced painful wounds of not having worth and value. The sources may vary, but the results are the same. They are insecurity and poor or low self-esteem. These wounds fester and result in attitudes, actions, and behaviors or fruit such as anger, depression, codependency, victimization, need for validation, performance, competition, comparisons, and self-loathing or hatred.

The Deceiver likes to use soul wounds to keep us in bondage. Sometimes the wounds begin in childhood and continue for a lifetime if we allow it. He created the devastation and continues to pour salt into our already wounded heart. It becomes a life lyric.

God see me as a workmanship. The word "workmanship" is the same word for poetry. This speaks of an artisan creating a beautiful piece of art. A masterpiece, symphony, and woven tapestry created to bring glory to the Lord. We are sculpted to reflect His image. The image we now reflect is Christ.

Many of us, including myself, are quick to criticize our appearance, skills, abilities, weaknesses, or faults. We can quickly identify every flaw we see in a mirror. Our weaknesses appear as neon signs over our heads flashing all negativity for the world to see. Instead of self-hate, how about some self-love? I am not talking about vanity or pride in our own abilities or appearance. If God really sees me as a workmanship or a beautiful poem, who am I to disagree?

How about asking the Holy Spirit to convict me when I put myself down? Paul repeatedly said he doesn't boast in his abilities. He counted them as rubbish in comparison to Christ. How about dumping the critical confessions and speaking what God says?

God sees me as a crown of glory. Again, we are royalty. We are no longer slaves, but heir of God with Christ (see Gal. 4:7). Even though we are born-again, and we understand theologically we are born into a heavenly royal family, many still operate with a "pauper" mentality. A pauper is an impoverished person. This mindset is based upon a lie of "never enough."

> *You shall also be a crown of glory, In the hand of the Lord,*
> *And a royal diadem In the hand of your God. Is. 62: 3*

God sees me not as forsaken. Despite our trials and circumstances that we experience in life, God will never abandon us or leave us or forsake us. Rom. 8:39 tells us that nothing can separate us from God's love.

> *You shall no longer be termed Forsaken, nor shall your*
> *land any more be termed Desolate; But you shall be called*
> *Hephzibah, and your land Beulah; For the Lord delights in*
> *you, And your land shall be married. Isa. 62:4*

It is tempting to think God has abandoned us in the midst of our difficulties. My senses tells me God is nowhere to be found. My flesh sounds the warning bell of being deserted. Yet Rom. 8:39, tells us that nothing will separate us from God's love.

> *nor height nor depth, nor any other created thing, shall be*
> *able to separate us from the love of God which is in Christ*
> *Jesus our Lord. Rom. 8:39*

We are not desolate, deserted, or abandoned. Our hope is in the everlasting covenant made for all eternity through the precious blood of Jesus. We stand on God's promises. We stand on His goodness and mercy, despite what we see and feel.

We turn our eyes off the circumstances and onto the author and finisher of our faith. We stand on His promises that He will finish what He began. He remains steadfast in His love for us. Our trial does not limit God's love for us. He is using them to fashion us into the image of His Son.

God sees me as chosen. What an incredible blessing to know that we have been selected because of Jesus for special privileges and blessings. We have been handpicked to represent Him and His kingdom. We have been chosen to receive grace, forgiveness, and redemption. He died for the whole world, but our salvation is an individual choice. Jesus is the way, truth, and life, and no one comes to the Father but through Jesus.

God sees me as justified. "Justified" is a legal term signifying to acquit or declare righteous or show to be righteous. Our sin made us guilty, and we all fell short of God's glory. Through the precious blood of Jesus our past sins have all been forgiven! He has made us righteous. That is right standing with God. Too many of us act and believe that God still sees our sins, weaknesses, failures, and mistakes. We allow shame and condemnation to overrule God's amazing justification. Our mistakes continually flash before us.

Of course, *The Deceiver* is relentless in reminding us of our failures and shortcomings. Condemnation is his language. Shame and guilt are the tools he uses to minimize everything God has done. He wants us to live in defeat rather than in victory through Jesus's death and resurrection. Remember Rom. 8:1?

> *There is therefore now no condemnation to those who are*
> *in Christ Jesus, who do not walk according to the flesh, but*
> *according to the Spirit. Rom. 8:1*

> *for all have sinned and fall short of the glory of God, being*
> *justified freely by His grace through the redemption that*
> *is in Christ Jesus, whom God set forth as a propitiation by*
> *His blood, through faith, to demonstrate His righteousness,*
> *because in His forbearance God had passed over the sins that*
> *were previously committed, to demonstrate at the present*
> *time His righteousness, that He might be just and the justifier*
> *of the one who has faith in Jesus. Rom. 3: 23–26*

New Identity = New Position

What is position?

A position is where someone or something is located or has been put. Our new identity has resulted in a new location! God has placed us in Christ. He has given us a new standing or level of importance in God's kingdom. We got a major upgrade, promotion with our new position in Christ!

How does God really see me?

If we are born-again, then God sees us as a son or daughter and as a joint heir with Christ. Since we are adopted, we are His children. Our Father is the King of Kings. So, we are royalty! We are a part of His family! We are no longer orphans, slaves, or outcasts. Our new position resulted in becoming a joint heir with Christ.

> *And because you are sons, God has sent forth the Spirit of His Son into your hearts, crying out, "Abba, Father!" Therefore, you are no longer a slave but a son, and if a son, then an heir of God through Christ.* Gal. 4:6–7

> *having predestined us to adoption as sons by Jesus Christ to Himself, according to the good pleasure of His will.* Eph. 1:5 *and if children, then heirs—heirs of God and joint heirs with Christ, if indeed we suffer with Him, that we may also be glorified together.* Romans 8:17

God sees me as accepted in *The Beloved*. We don't need to be afraid of rejection. We can have security in God's unconditional love and acceptance. The same acceptance and love the Father has for Jesus, He has for you! He will not compare or disapprove of you. You are perfect in His eyes. Remember, He now sees you through His Beloved Son.

To the praise of the glory of His grace, by which He made us
accepted in The Beloved. Eph. 1:6.

God sees me as reconciled. Sin created a separation from God. There was enmity between God and us. We were enemies and alienated from Him. We were unknown to the covenants of God. Through Jesus there is no more separation! We have been brought near by the blood of Jesus.

And you, who once were alienated and enemies in your mind
by wicked works, yet now He has reconciled in the body of His
flesh through death, to present you holy, and blameless, and
above reproach in His sight. Col 1:21–22

For He Himself is our peace, who has made both one, and has
broken down the middle wall of separation, having abolished
in His flesh the enmity, that is, the law of commandments
contained in ordinances, so as to create in Himself one new
man from the two, thus making peace, and that He might
reconcile them both to God in one body through the cross,
thereby putting to death the enmity. Eph. 2:14–16

God sees me as raised with Christ. Since we were baptized in His death and resurrection, we are raised with Christ. Our flesh lives here on the earth, but our spirit is seated with Christ. What does that mean? The old man or flesh is fighting against our new man. Paul sums it up in Romans 7 when he said that he did not do what he want to and did what he did not want to do, but the life he lives is through Christ by faith.

But God, who is rich in mercy, because of His great love with which He loved us, even when we were dead in trespasses, made us alive together with Christ (by grace you have been saved), and raised us up together, and made us sit together in the heavenly places in Christ Jesus, that in the ages to come He might show the exceeding riches of His grace in His kindness toward us in Christ Jesus. For by grace you have been saved through faith, and that not of yourselves; it is the gift of God, Eph. 2: 4–8

If then you were raised with Christ, seek those things which are above, where Christ is, sitting at the right hand of God.
Colossians 3:1

This shows how valuable we are and how important we are. It is because of the richness of His mercy we have been raised with Christ! We have the promise that in the age to come, God will show us, His beloved children, the exceeding riches of His grace and kindness toward us!

God sees me as complete in Him. We now lack nothing! We have everything we need in Christ. All of our needs are met through Christ Jesus. I am asking God to reveal the richness of this verse to you. We think we need more success, wealth, education, or

influence or a bigger house or new car to be complete. That is a lie.
None of these things will make me feel whole or complete,

and you are complete in Him, who is the head of all
principality and power. Col. 2:10

For we are glad when we are weak, and you are strong. And
this also we pray, that you may be made complete. 2 Cor. 13:9

make you complete in every good work to do His will,
working in you what is well pleasing in His sight, through
Jesus Christ, to whom be glory forever and ever. Amen.
Heb. 13:21

God sees me as justified. To justify is to declare righteous, acquit,
and show to be righteous. Think about this: an acquittal signifies
that a prosecutor failed to prove his or her case beyond a reason-
able doubt. Our crime was our sin. We were guilty, but God has
now declared we are innocent!

Our faith in Jesus's salvation makes us in right standing with
God. I cannot do anything to plead my innocence. There are no plea
bargains or reduced sentencing. I am guilty as charged. However,
through Jesus, He took my place and received my sentencing.

Being justified freely by His grace through the redemption that
is in Christ Jesus, Rom. 3:24

Therefore, having been justified by faith, we have peace with God through our Lord Jesus Christ. Rom. 5:1

Moreover, whom He predestined, these He also called; whom He called, these He also justified; and whom He justified, and these He also glorified. Rom. 8:30

God sees me as forgiven. We have been abundantly pardoned and relieved of the burden of sin. There are no accounts and no records of our past mistakes. No matter how big or small, they have been wiped clean. There is no sin that the sacrificial blood cannot erase!

Isn't it awesome that we don't need a high priest to offer blood sacrifice to get forgiveness? We simply access the Throne of Grace and through Jesus. The Bible tells us if we confess our sin, God is faithful and just to forgive. Our sin is forgotten, wiped clean. God doesn't remember our sin.

Therefore, I say to you, her sins, which are many, are forgiven, for she loved much. But to whom little is forgiven, the same loves little. Luke 7:47

Blessed are those whose lawless deeds are forgiven, and whose sins are covered. Rom. 4:7

And you, being dead in your trespasses and the uncircumcision of your flesh, He has made alive together with Him, having forgiven you all trespasses. Col: 2:13

New Identity= New Privilege

Our identity in Christ grants us incredible privileges gained only through His salvation. These gifts have been obtained through the powerful blood of Jesus. These rights or favors have only been bestowed upon us as joint heirs in Christ.

I have the privilege to access the Throne of Grace. Have you ever gone to your father for help or advice? When I was a teenager, asking for minor things like the car keys seemed huge. My needs grew as I became an adult.

When I was a single mom, I had need of finances, transportation, and a place to stay. My dad generously provided for our needs. I did not ask often, because I was afraid of asking too many questions. I did not want to be a pest. There is some residual fear of rejection on my part.

However, we have a heavenly Father who never grows weary or troubled with our petitions. It makes Him happy to give good gifts to His children. We can just walk into the throne room anytime! The door is never locked because it is not even shut. It is wide open. We have access to our Father every moment of every day.

We never are a pest to God. He is never too busy! At no time is it ever inconvenient to go into the heavenly throne room of God. We can be confident that He will hear us. He said in His Word to come boldly, so we can just go on in and speak to our Father. He is our Abba, our Father. He is our Daddy God. He is not like earthly fathers who have flaws. He is in His own category of a perfect Father.

We have been given so much more than the keys to the family car. We have been given the keys to the kingdom, unlocking blessings, answered prayer, healing, restoration, and transformation. We believe God and exercise our faith and our rights as children of God. We are told to ask, and it shall be given unto us. Of course, we ask in accordance to His Word and His will.

When we go to our heavenly Father, we can trust He has the best answer for us. It may be a yes, a no, or not now. He sees the beginning from the end. He knows what to give us, so what are you waiting for? Walk on in! You can boldly access the throne room of grace. Your Father is waiting to meet you this very moment.

Let us then fearlessly and confidently and boldly draw near to the throne of grace (the throne of God's unmerited favor to us sinners) that we may receive mercy (for our failures) and find grace to help in good time for every need (appropriate help and well-timed help, coming just when we need it).

Heb. 4:16 Amp

We have the privilege to be a royal priesthood. We are royalty since we are children of the King of Kings and joint heirs with Christ. As priests we have the privilege of bringing sacrifices of worship and adoration. We get to worship Him because He is worthy. He is so deserving of sincere respect, admiration, and esteem.

As a royal priesthood, we have the privilege of offer praise and thanksgiving. The Alpha and Omega, Jehovah, Yaweh, or Adonai delight in our praises! God takes great pleasure, happiness, joy, and gladness in us! He loves when we come into His presence with worship and adoration. He inhabits our praises. There is sweet fellowship in worship.

I have the privilege of worship. We have so many reasons to worship the Lord. Not just on Sundays, but he is deserving of daily worship. Here are a few reasons:

- God's goodness, power, love, faithfulness is reason to worship
- He inhabits, dwells, and resides in our praise
- Many battles in the Old Testament were won through praise. 2 Chron. 20
- It takes our mind off our problems
- Faith will rise when we remind ourselves of God's power, love, etc.
- God can speak to us during worship
- God deserves our worship
- We get to bless God!

We have the privilege to prayer and intercede. Because we are royal priests we can now come boldly to His throne and intercede for others, our city, and our nation and see God move. Our prayers are sweet incense to God. He welcomes our prayers. Transformation occurs when we couple our prayers with persistence, faith, and God's Word.

> *The effective (successful, valuable), fervent (impassioned,*
> *burning) prayer of a righteous man avails much.*
> James 5:17 Amp

Because of our righteousness in Christ Jesus, we can passionately intercede in accordance with God's Word and will, and we will see answered prayers. Don't underestimate the power of your prayers. Be bold in your prayers. Be confident! Pray the Word of God!

Therefore, we can enter boldly enter in and bless the Lord with our worship, adoration, and praise. We get the privilege of ushering in His presence. We can have sweet communion with our heavenly Father. We can access the Throne of Grace because of the blood of Jesus! He sees you as acceptable and welcomes us into His presence.

New Identity = New Abilities

Our identity in Christ has granted us incredible new abilities. Isn't that awesome! We can develop, exercise, and strengthen all things in and through the Holy Spirit. He is the one who created heaven and earth, created something from nothing, put the heaven and sea in its place. He lives inside of us the instant we ask Christ into our heart.

- Accomplishment
- Adeptness
- Adroitness
- Aptitude
- Capability
- Capacity
- Cleverness
- Competence
- Deftness
- Dexterity
- Expertise
- Facility
- Faculty
- Finesse
- Flair
- Genius
- Gift
- Knack
- Know-how!
- Mastery
- Means
- Potential
- Potentiality
- Power
- Proficiency
- Prowess

- Qualification
- Resources
- Savoir faire
- Skill
- Skillfulness
- Talent
- Wherewithal

Testimonies:

Esther had a lifetime of drug abuse. When she met my pastor's wife, she couldn't think or write. Pastor Pat told her to read the Word out loud. The Word and Holy Spirit totally healed her mind, and she ended up getting a master's degree and was brilliant!

Ann wanted to learn to play worship music on the guitar. The Holy Spirit was her teacher, and now she leads worship!

We are baptized in Jesus's death and resurrection and have the same Holy Spirit that raised Christ from the dead. We can do all things through Christ Jesus who strengthens us. Remember, the key is in Jesus. In our own strength we cannot do anything. But through Him in the power of the Holy Spirit and the power of His Word we can do all things.

Here are some of the new abilities

God sees me as more than a conqueror. I am more than a conqueror through Jesus, and in Him and by Him I can defeat, subdue, or overcome anything in my life. I am victorious in Christ. Limitations, obstacles can no longer keep me from my victory.

Yet in all these things we are more than conquerors through Him who loved us. Rom. 8:37

God sees me as able to walk worthy of Him. We are sinful, fallible, and we make mistakes. Without the Holy Spirit and salvation no one can make God happy and satisfied. Stop trying to please God. You already do because of Jesus. Prayer, worship, and attending church are important. They will not add one more ounce to God's satisfaction, love, or acceptance, toward us. We can walk worthy of the Lord, fully pleasing Him in all things, and we make God happy and satisfied!

God gave His absolute best. And in His Son Jesus we've been made complete, perfect, redeemed, holy, and blameless. I think it insults God when we try to add our "religious" activities to the redemptive work of Jesus. I cannot add anything to make Him love or approve of me. I am complete in Him.

I can walk worthy of the Lord, fully pleasing Him in all things, bearing fruit in every good work and increasing in the knowledge of God. Col 1:10

God sees me as delivered from the power of darkness. Darkness has no control over me anymore. So, I can choose if I am going to allow it to control me. It is a battle, but Jesus already won, and I can be victorious through him if I want victory.

God sees us able to bear fruit in every good work. The Holy Spirit will produce His fruit of love, joy, peace, long-suffering or endurance, kindness, goodness, faithfulness, and self-control (see Gal 5:22). When we display this type of fruit, then we are led by the Holy Spirit. And He's in control.

When we don't, we are under the flesh, and the flesh is against God and cannot please God. When the Holy Spirit can fully operate in our lives, and we are yielded to Him, His fruit becomes a springboard to bring the kingdom of God to earth.

I get in my flesh a lot. I make mistakes, I blow it, and I fail. I used to allow The Deceiver to bring condemnation and shame. He would relentlessly replay every mistake and tell me I was a failure. He would accuse me that I was not worthy. He would tell me it was too late, and I wouldn't change. You know he was right, expect for one important fact. Because I am in Christ, there is no condemnation. Now I don't allow condemnation to overtake me; there's no condemnation or shame. According to Romans 8:1, there is no condemnation for those that are in Christ Jesus.

God sees me with the ability to increase in the knowledge of God. This isn't more theology or book knowledge. The biblical definition of knowledge means "putting together, quickness of apprehension, the critical faculty apprehension, intelligently assessing a situation. The Holy Spirit dwells in us and will give us wisdom if we ask!

My testimony:

When I was in graduate school, I had to write a paper on law and ethics. Since we only had four weeks per course, I had to start writing it the first week of class. I had no clue of law and ethics at that point. I asked the Holy Spirit to help me. He did, and I got an "A." I was thankful, but surprised and told Him, "Wow, you really do know law and ethics!" Silly of me to be surprised; after all, He had the knowledge to create everything.

Example:

My wonderful husband has a technical job and is always asking the Holy Spirit for wisdom. God will speak to him in technical terms, parts, and systems. People are always amazed how he figures out most problems so quickly!

> *For this reason, we also, since the day we heard it, do not cease to pray for you, and to ask that you may be filled with the knowledge of His will in all wisdom and spiritual understanding.* Col. 1:9

I've been a Christian for over forty years, and I can honestly say there's so much more I want to know about Him. I am so grateful for the Holy Spirit and His incredible wisdom, both practical and spiritual. I am so thankful He is revealing more of Jesus to me every day.

God sees me with the ability to overcome fear. As I mentioned earlier, fear was the first response of Adam and Eve when sin occurred. Fear is common in all people. Phobias, anxiety, avoiding, hiding, panic, apprehension, nervousness are all expressions of fear.

For God has not given us a spirit of fear, but of power and of love and of a sound mind. 2 Tim. 1:7

Example:

Mary had a huge fear of never getting into Hollywood. She believed everyone who told her she would never make it. Failure was always just around the corner. Despite her twenty-year pursuit, her dream had never materialized. After she learned her identity in Christ, she is fearless. This gal who was insecure, afraid, and timid is bolder than a lion and absolutely confident in Christ.

In conclusion, the big question of who am I? has been asked throughout history. Poets, philosophers, and psychologists have contemplated this question for days, weeks, and even years. Behind this question lie deeper questions such as

- Am I really loved?
- What is my significance?
- Where do I belong?
- Who am I?

Through our relationship with *The Beloved*, these four questions have been answered with deep, meaningful answers. We are loved by Him. He has determined our significance, worth, and value. We are defined by Him. We belong eternally to Him as joint heirs. We have been adopted as His children.

* * *

Dance of Freedom

Let's take the four foundational steps and apply them to the Dance of Identity. Each step is important to the entire Dance of Freedom. Take some time to pray and ask the Holy Spirit to help you and reveal truth. God's truth will set you free.

And you shall know the truth, and the truth shall make you free. John 8:32

Foundational Step #1: Dance of Awareness

The Dance of Awareness is important because it helps us to understand the relationship between our fruit (attitudes, actions, emotions), our trunk (beliefs or lyrics), and our soil (relationships, events, circumstances).

Fruit: Circle the fruit on your tree:

- Anxiety
- Comparisons
- Fears
- Insecurity
- Pride
- Self-hate
- What is my value?
- Where do I belong?
- Where do I find approval?
- Who am I?

Prayer:

Father,

You see the fruit that is on my tree, and I desire Your fruit. Holy Spirit, release Your power, love, and grace in my life. Transform me from the inside out. Let Your truth set me free. Let Your love penetrate my heart and soul so I will know my identity in You.

How misplaced identity affects our roots and soil

As misplaced identity passes through our family tree, it makes its way into our soil and roots. It causes us to constantly look for validation of our identity. We constantly are looking for someone to tell us we are loved. Am I valued? Where do I belong?

What sources of misplaced identity are in your roots or soil? Circle all that apply:

- Comparisons
- Fears
- Focus on achievements
- Insecurity
- Performance
- Pride
- Questions of worth and value
- Self-hate
- Where do I belong?
- Where do I find approval?

Prayer:

Father,

You see the roots of misplaced identity. They have left a big hole in my heart only You can fill. You can answer my heart's desire to know who I am. You have given me your approval, and I belong to You. Heal the wounds of misplaced identity. Help me not to strive for the world's approval because I already have Yours.

What is my root? Circle what applies to you:

The roots are the channels that extract nutrients from the soil and nourish the entire tree. Our soil can be culture, relationships, how we were raised, experiences, etc. The soil feeds our trunk or beliefs, then produces fruit. HOWEVER, we can change our soil through the Word of God, resulting in good fruit such as peace, love, joy, self-control, patience, goodness, healing, deliverance, healthy relationships, etc.

- Codependency
- Controlling relationships
- Emotional, sexual, or physical abuse
- Insecurity
- Low self esteem
- Patterns of feeling powerless, helpless, victimized

Foundational Step #2: Dance of the Word

Words have great power. They have the power to shape, influence, build, destroy, plant, and bring things into life. Think of the words you have heard. It doesn't matter if they came from people, *The Deceiver*, or yourself. You were influenced and affected by their power.

Circle the words of misplaced identity you have heard:

- You have no worth and value
- Who are you?
- You are a failure
- You are a mistake
- You are inadequate
- You are insignificant

- You are misfit
- You are not loved
- You are small
- You don't belong

Write down other ones:

_____

_____

_____

Prayer:

Father,

You see the words of misplaced identity that have impacted me. You know the destruction it has caused. Forgive me for listening to them. I am tired of the world telling me who I am or determining my worth and value. You have adopted me as Your child and declared that I am a joint heir with Christ. I am a part of Your family. Help me to cling to Your Word.

Foundational Step #3: Dance of Lyrics

Life lyrics cause us to respond in certain ways. Music and lyrics create "priming." This is when a person is exposed to certain stimuli such as words, lyrics, or surroundings, and their subconscious mind is activated. Once activated, the person's behavior, actions, or attitudes come out in ways that are consistent with the stimulus without awareness of why they are behaving in that manner.

Circle all the life lyrics that apply:

- I am a failure
- I am bound by fear
- I am small
- I do not know who I am
- I don't know where I belong
- I feel alone
- I have to perform
- I was a mistake
- My value is determined by others

Prayer:

Father,

You see my destructive lyrics I have believed. Please forgive me for believing them more than Your truth. Holy Spirit, release Your power, love, and grace in my life. Transform me from the inside out. Let my heart hear You sing over my life. Untangle me from these lies and help me to soar on wings of eagles.

Jerusalem will be told: Don't be afraid. Dear Zion,
don't despair. Your God is present among you, a strong
Warrior there to save you. Happy to have you back,

He'll calm you with his love and delight you with his songs.

Zeph. 3:17 The Msg. Bible

The Beloved's Lyrics (adapted from scripture):

Circle the ones that apply to you: IMPORTANT TO READ THESE LYRICS OUT LOUD UNTIL YOU BELIEVE IN YOUR HEART. (Initially, you may not believe what you are speaking, but FAITH COMES BY HEARING). God's Word will not come back to Him void but will fulfill its intention.

- My identity is based upon God's unconditional love, according to Eph. 1:6
- My identity is not rooted in spirit of fear but of power, of love, and of a sound mind. 2 Tim 1:7

Prayer:

Holy Spirit,

Thank You that You are the power that raised Christ from the dead and You are working in me. As I read and speak Your Word over me, let the reality of my new identity heal transform, renew, regenerate my heart and life. Let these new lyrics produce the fruit of Your righteousness in my life.

Foundational Step #4: Dance of Forgiveness

Forgiveness of self and others is essential to learning how to dance with *The Beloved*. Unforgiveness impacts our spiritual, physical, and emotional health. It keeps us in prison and subject to being tormented by *The Deceiver*.

Who determined your identity? Parents, teachers, coaches, boss, coworker, or spouse?

List their name here:

_____

_____

_____

Prayer:

Father,

I choose to forgive because I know it will set me free. I choose forgiveness because it is what You want me to do. I do not want to be tormented by The Enemy (The Deceiver) any longer. I want out of the prison within my soul. I do not want to be his puppet and controlled by bitterness, anger, or resentment. Help me when I do not want to forgive. Wash my heart clean and remove the stain of bitterness from my heart.

* * *

Dance with *The Beloved*

Precious and The Beloved begin to dance. She sees the hall of mirrors and starts to feel the same panic and worry like before. She listens to The Beloved as He sings a love song to her. He reminds her of her identity which is rooted in His love, grace, and covenant.

The mirrors are no longer empty frames, but rather she sees new images of herself through the eyes of The Beloved. She sees value, strength, worth, and assurance. Peace for the first time fills her heart as she realizes she belongs to Him.

* * *

Dance your way to freedom! Envision yourself as the dancer.
https://mariplanklifecoach.com/
dance-of-identity-overcoming-mistaken-identity/

References

1.Vallotton, Kris, The Supernatural Ways of Royalty, Shippensburg, Destiny Image Publishers,